Contents

List of resources	3
Introduction	4
How to use the CD-ROM	5

Going to France — PAGE 7
Notes on the CD-ROM resources	8
Notes on the photocopiable pages	16
Photocopiable pages	18

Living in Scotland — PAGE 25
Notes on the CD-ROM resources	26
Notes on the photocopiable pages	35
Photocopiable pages	36

A village in The Gambia — PAGE 41
Notes on the CD-ROM resources	42
Notes on the photocopiable pages	53
Photocopiable pages	55

Train ride through Europe — PAGE 61
Notes on the CD-ROM resources	62
Notes on the photocopiable pages	72
Photocopiable pages	74

Licence

IMPORTANT – PERMITTED USE AND WARNINGS – READ CAREFULLY BEFORE USING

Copyright in the software contained in this CD-ROM and in its accompanying material belongs to Scholastic Limited. All rights reserved. © Scholastic Ltd, 2005.

The material contained on this CD-ROM may only be used in the context for which it was intended in *Ready Resources*. School site use is permitted only within the school of the purchaser of the book and CD-ROM. Permission to download images is given for purchasers only and not for borrowers from any lending service. Any further use of the material contravenes Scholastic Ltd's copyright and that of other rights holders.

Save for these purposes, or as expressly authorised in the accompanying materials, the software may not be copied, reproduced, used, sold, licensed, transferred, exchanged, hired, or exported in whole or in part or in any manner or form without the prior written consent of Scholastic Ltd. Any such unauthorised use or activities are prohibited and may give rise to civil liabilities and criminal prosecutions.

This CD-ROM has been tested for viruses at all stages of its production. However, we recommend that you run virus-checking software on your computer systems at all times. Scholastic Ltd cannot accept any responsibility for any loss, disruption or damage to your data or your computer system that may occur as a result of using either the CD-ROM or the data held on it.

IF YOU ACCEPT THE ABOVE CONDITIONS YOU MAY PROCEED TO USE THIS CD-ROM

Text © Liz Lewis and Margaret Mackintosh
© 2005 Scholastic Ltd

Published by Scholastic Ltd, Villiers House,
Clarendon Avenue, Leamington Spa,
Warwickshire CV32 5PR

Printed by Bell & Bain Ltd, Glasgow

1234567890   5678901234

British Library Cataloguing-in-Publication Data
A catalogue record for this book is available from the British Library.

ISBN 0-439-97194-2
ISBN 978-0439-97194-2

Visit our website at
www.scholastic.co.uk

CD developed in association with
Footmark Media Ltd

Authors
Liz Lewis and Margaret Mackintosh

Editor
Sally Gray

Project Editor
Wendy Tse

Assistant Editors
Aileen Lalor and Kim Vernon

Series Designer
Joy Monkhouse

Designer
Erik Ivens

Cover photographs
© Photodisc
© Franz Waldhaeusl/Alamy
Thistle © Andy Horton
© Photodisc via SODA

Acknowledgements

Extracts from the National Curriculum for England © Crown copyright material is reproduced with the permission of the Controller of HMSO and the Queen's Printer for Scotland. Extracts from Programmes of Study from The National Curriculum reproduced under the terms of HMSO Guidance Note 8. © Qualifications and Curriculum Authority.

Wes Magee for the use of 'The Harbour Wall' © Wes Magee.

Every effort has been made to trace copyright holders and the publishers apologise for any omissions.

Due to the nature of the web, the publisher cannot guarantee the content or links of any of the websites referred to. It is the responsibility of the reader to assess the suitability of websites.

The rights of Liz Lewis and Margaret Mackintosh to be identified as the authors of this work have been asserted by them in accordance with the Copyright, Designs and Patents Act 1988.

All rights reserved. This book is sold subject to the condition that it shall not, by way of trade or otherwise, be lent, hired out or otherwise circulated without the publisher's prior consent in any form of binding or cover other than that in which it is published and without a similar condition, including this condition, being imposed upon the subsequent purchaser.
   No part of this publication may be reproduced, stored in a retrieval system, or transmitted, in any form or by any means, electronic, mechanical, photocopying, recording or otherwise, without the prior permission of the publisher. This book remains copyright, although permission is granted to copy pages where indicated for classroom distribution and use only in the school which has purchased the book and in accordance with the CLA licensing agreement. Photocopying permission is given only for purchasers and not for borrowers of books from any lending service.

 Made with Macromedia is a trademark of Macromedia, Inc. Director ® Copyright © 1984-2000 Macromedia, Inc.

 QuickTime and the QuickTime logo are trademarks used under license. The QuickTime logo is registered in the US and other countries.

List of resources on the CD-ROM

The page numbers refer to the teachers' notes provided in this book.

Going to France

Map of cross-channel routes	8
Dover marina	8
Seacat ferry	8
Leaving England	9
Port of Calais	9
Pont de Normandie	10
Honfleur harbour	10
Eating out in Honfleur	11
At the greengrocer's	11
Bayeux tapestry: Leaving France, Crossing the Channel, Landing at Pevensey	11
Journey to Paris	12
Video: the Arc de Triomphe	12
The Paris Metro	13
Walking in Paris	14
Notre Dame Cathedral	14
Sacré Coeur Basilica	15
The Eiffel Tower	15
Tuileries Gardens	15
Eurostar	16

Living in Scotland

Scotland in the British Isles	26
Aerial view of Edinburgh	26
Pictorial map of central Edinburgh	27
Daisy and James' local area	27
Daisy going to school	28
James at nursery	28
James at lunchtime	28
Shopping on the Royal Mile	28
James at Edinburgh Zoo, Zebra	29
Map of the Royal Botanic Gardens	29
Princes Street: busy street, shop fronts	30
Scottish National Portrait Gallery: outside, inside	30
Edinburgh Castle	31
The Forth rail bridge, The Forth road bridge	31
Winter sports at Aviemore	32
Urquhart Castle at Loch Ness, Tourist shop	32
Dancing at the Highland Games	33
Scottish music: Catherine-Ann MacPhee	33
Hogmanay in Edinburgh	34
Highland cattle	34
Aberdeen docks	34

A village in The Gambia

Lamin Darboe's family	42
Where is The Gambia?	42
Pictorial map of western Gambia	42
Map of Mandinari	43
Lamin's compound	44
Rohey's kitchen	44
The women's gardens	45
Rice harvesting	45
A mosque in Mandinari	46
Mandinari nursery school	46
Mandinari primary school	46
Nicola and Kadi ready for school	47
Water supply	47
Shopping in Mandinari	48
Mandinari's river and creek	48
Mandinari in the rain	49
Shopping in Serekunda, Serekunda's indoor market	49
Getting around	50
Being a Muslim	50
Banjul	51
Banjul street scene	51
The River Gambia	52
Children playing	52
Drums	53
Audio: Kora music	53

Train ride through Europe

Map of Europe	62
Dutch canal and bicycle, Dutch houseboat	62
Dutch houses	63
Windmill and windturbine, Dutch countryside	63
Map of the upper River Rhine	64
The Rhine Valley, Barge on the River Rhine	64
Strasbourg	65
The Rhine Falls	65
Map of the Bernese Oberland	66
Walking in the mountains, Hang-gliding	66
Cogwheel railway, Cable car	67
Swiss village	68
Jungfraubahn	68
Eiger Glacier	69
Aerial view of Venice	69
The Grand Canal, Waterbus	70
Water ambulance	70
Video: A gondola ride	71
Living in Venice, Shopping in Venice	71

INTRODUCTION

This book and CD-ROM support the teaching and learning set out in the QCA Scheme of Work for geography in Years 1 and 2. The CD provides a large bank of visual and aural resources. The book provides teachers' notes, background information, ideas for discussion and activities to accompany the CD resources, along with photocopiable pages to support the teaching. All have been specifically chosen to meet the requirements for resources listed in the QCA units for Years 1 and 2. Some additional resources and ideas have also been included to enable teachers to develop and broaden these areas of study if they wish. These include activity sheets to help children clarify their thinking or record what they find out.

The resources and activities are not intended to provide a structure for teaching in themselves, but are designed to give a basis for discussion and activities which focus on the knowledge, skills and understanding required by the National Curriculum for geography. The children are encouraged to develop key skills such as observing, questioning, describing, sorting, sequencing, comparing and explaining.

Graphicacy is one of the key skills in geography and it covers all forms of pictorial communication of spatial information: ground-level photographs, oblique and vertical aerial photographs, diagrams, signs and symbols, and maps of all sorts – from pictorial to Ordnance Survey. Maps and their conventional use of plan view are important in geography, but children see their world from eye-level. There is a large conceptual leap between eye-level and plan (aerial) view so children can be helped to make sense of, and understand, the relationship between horizontal and vertical viewpoints by the use of intermediate perspectives, that is, views taken from a range of oblique angles.

Links with other subjects

Literacy
There are a number of close links between the units covered in this book and work on literacy. The discussion activities contribute directly to the requirements for speaking and listening. There is considerable opportunity for the children to develop their independent writing skills as they produce leaflets or write simple captions using the word cards. Images from the CD could be printed to stimulate independent writing, or to illustrate it.

Maths
Skills such as counting, measuring, matching, ordering and sequencing are essential to both geography and maths. Measuring skills are fostered when children calculate distances, and they learn to tell the time by working out how long journeys take. Data collection and creating bar charts and simple graphs are excellent geographical tools and can aid explanations of the dynamics of city life, as well as providing visual information about people and places.

Design and technology
There are many opportunities in the children's 'travels' in this book to learn about the workings of transport (from barges, ferries and bicycles to the underground Metro in Paris) and also bridges (in Scotland, France and the Rhine Valley). Several of the activities featured in this book involve the children in designing and making models, such as making model boats (page 35).

PSHE
Looking at the similarities and differences between their own lives and the lives of others in neighbouring countries as well as those in a far away place will help the children to gain an understanding and appreciation of other cultures.

Modern foreign languages
Although modern foreign language teaching is not a requirement at Key Stage 1, children are introduced to the concept of different languages in the study of selected European countries.

HOW TO USE THE CD-ROM

Windows NT users
If you use Windows NT you may see the following error message: 'The procedure entry point Process32First could not be located in the dynamic link library KERNEL32.dll'. Click on **OK** and the CD will autorun with no further problems.

Setting up your computer for optimal use
On opening, the CD will alert you if changes are needed in order to operate the CD at its optimal use. There are three changes you may be advised to make:

Viewing resources at their maximum screen size
To see images at their maximum screen size, your screen display needs to be set to 800 x 600 pixels. In order to adjust your screen size you will need to **Quit** the program.

If using a PC, open the **Control Panel**. Select **Display** and then **Settings**. Adjust the **Desktop Area** to 800 x 600 pixels. Click on **OK** and then restart the program.

If using a Mac, from the **Apple** menu select **Control Panels** and then **Monitors** to adjust the screen size.

Adobe Acrobat Reader
To print high-quality versions of images and to view and print the photocopiable pages on the CD you need **Adobe Acrobat Reader** installed on your computer. If you do not have it installed already, a version is provided on the CD. To install this version **Quit** the 'Ready Resources' program.

If using a PC, right-click on the **Start** menu on your desktop and choose **Explore**. Click on the + sign to the left of the CD drive entitled 'Ready Resources' and open the folder called 'Acrobat Reader Installer'. Run the program contained in this folder to install **Adobe Acrobat Reader**.

If using a Mac, double-click on the 'Ready Resources' icon on the desktop and on the 'Acrobat Reader Installer' folder. Run the program contained in this folder to install **Adobe Acrobat Reader**.

PLEASE NOTE: If you do not have **Adobe Acrobat Reader** installed, you will not be able to print high-quality versions of images, or to view or print photocopiable pages (although these are provided in this book and can be photocopied).

It is recommended that certain images, such as maps and aerial views, are viewed and printed in **Adobe Acrobat Reader** as it will be easier to focus on specific areas.

QuickTime
In order to view the videos and listen to the audio on this CD you will need to have **QuickTime version 5 or later** installed on your computer. The latest version is provided on the CD. If you choose to install this version, **Quit** the 'Ready Resources' program.

If using a PC, right-click on the **Start** menu on your desktop and choose **Explore**. Click on the + sign to the left of the CD drive that is entitled 'Ready Resources' and open the folder called 'QuickTime Installer'. Run the program contained in this folder to install **QuickTime**.

If using a Mac, double-click on the 'Ready Resources' CD icon on the desktop and then on the 'Acrobat Reader Installer' folder. Run the program contained in this folder to install **QuickTime**.

PLEASE NOTE: If you do not have **QuickTime** installed you will not be able to view the films.

Menu screen
▶ Click on the **Resource Gallery** of your choice to view the resources available under that topic.
▶ Click on **Complete Resource Gallery** to view all the resources available on the CD.
▶ Click on **Photocopiable Resources (PDF format)** to view a list of the photocopiables provided in this book.
▶ **Back:** click to return to the **opening screen**. Click **Continue** to move to the **Menu screen**.
▶ **Quit:** click **Quit** to close the menu program and progress to the **Quit screen**. If you quit from the **Quit screen** you will exit the CD. If you do not quit you will return to the **Menu screen**.

Resource Galleries
▶ **Help:** click **Help** to find support on accessing and using images.
▶ **Back to menu:** click here to return to the **Menu screen**.
▶ **Quit:** click here to move to the **Quit screen** – see **Quit** above.

HOW TO USE THE CD-ROM

Viewing images
Small versions of each image are shown in the Resource Gallery. Click and drag the slider on the slide bar to scroll through the images in the Resource Gallery, or click on the arrows to move the images frame by frame. Roll the pointer over an image to see the caption.
▶ Click on an image to view the screen-sized version of it.
▶ To return to the Resource Gallery click on **Back to Resource Gallery**.

Viewing videos
Click on the video icon of your choice in the Resource Gallery. In order to view the videos on this CD, you will need to have **QuickTime** installed on your computer (see 'Setting up your computer for optimal use' above).

Once at the video screen, use the buttons on the bottom of the video screen to operate the video. The slide bar can be used for a fast forward and rewind. To return to the Resource Gallery click on **Back to Resource Gallery**.

Listening to sound recordings
Click on the required sound icon. Use the buttons or the slide bar to hear the sound. A transcript will be displayed on the viewing screen where appropriate. To return to the Resource Gallery, click on **Back to Resource Gallery**.

Printing
Click on the image to view it (see 'Viewing images' above). There are two print options:

Print using Acrobat enables you to print a high-quality version of an image. Choosing this option means that the image will open as a read-only page in **Adobe Acrobat** and in order to access these files you will need to have already installed **Adobe Acrobat Reader** on your computer (see 'Setting up your computer for optimal use' above). To print the selected resource, select **File** and then **Print**. Once you have printed the resource **minimise** or **close** the Adobe screen using — or X in the top right-hand corner of the screen. Return to the Resource Gallery by clicking on **Back to Resource Gallery**.

Simple print enables you to print a lower-quality version of the image without the need to use **Adobe Acrobat Reader**. Select the image and click on the **Simple print** option. After printing, click on **Back to Resource Gallery**.

Slideshow presentation
If you would like to present a number of resources without having to return to the Resource Gallery and select a new image each time, you can compile a slideshow. Click on the + tabs at the top of each image in the Resource Gallery you would like to include in your presentation (pictures, sound and video can be included). It is important that you click on the images in the order in which you would like to view them (a number will appear on each tab to confirm the order). If you would like to change the order, click on **Clear slideshow** and begin again.

Once you have selected your images – up to a maximum of 20 – click on **Play slideshow** and you will be presented with the first of your selected resources. To move to the next selection in your slideshow click on **Next slide**, to see a previous resource click on **Previous slide**. You can end your slideshow presentation at any time by clicking on **Resource Gallery**. Your slideshow selection will remain selected until you **Clear slideshow** or return to the **Menu screen**.

Viewing on an interactive whiteboard or data projector
Resources can be viewed directly from the CD. To make viewing easier for a whole class, use a large monitor, data projector or interactive whiteboard. For group, paired or individual work, the resources can be viewed from the computer screen.

Photocopiable resources (PDF format)
To view or print a photocopiable resource page, click on the required title in the list and the page will open as a read-only page in **Adobe Acrobat**. In order to access these files you will need to have already installed **Adobe Acrobat Reader** on your computer (see 'Setting up your computer for optimal use' above). To print the selected resource select **File** and then **Print**. Once you have printed the resource **minimise** or **close** the Adobe screen using — or X in the top right-hand corner of the screen. This will take you back to the list of PDF files. To return to the **Menu screen**, click on **Back**.

GOING TO FRANCE

Content and skills
This chapter links to Units 5 and 24 of the QCA scheme of work for Geography at Key Stage 1, 'Where in the world is Barnaby Bear?' and 'Passport to the world', respectively. The 'Going to France' Gallery on the CD-ROM, together with the teachers' notes and photocopiable pages in this chapter, can be used when teaching these units. For example, when teaching Unit 5, some of the resources in this book could be adapted easily to link to travels involving Barnaby Bear – particularly the 'Barnaby Goes to Brittany' materials.

This chapter encourages the children to think about where places are, what places are like, and how they are similar to and different from our own country and locality. Central to this are the opportunities provided to develop geographical skills such as visual literacy through observation of a range of features and environments from pictures and video clips, maps, plans and other secondary sources of information. The materials encourage familiarity with a wide range of geographical vocabulary.

The teachers' notes offer suggestions for discussion of the resources as well as ways of using them as a whole class, in smaller groups or as individuals. Some of the activities link with other areas of the curriculum. There are also links to history, technology, art, PSHE and citizenship in many of the activities. Simple French vocabulary is introduced in contexts familiar to the children, such as eating out and shopping, which will be particularly valuable where schools are involved in primary MFL work.

The underlying rationale of the work is to support the development of children's curiosity about a neighbouring part of Europe so that wherever possible the activities encourage the children to ask and answer questions and develop an enquiring approach to their learning.

Resources on the CD-ROM
The CD-ROM offers a range of images of France focusing on two locations – Honfleur, an attractive small port in Normandy; and the capital city, Paris. Some care has been taken to avoid presenting only stereotypical views of French life. Therefore, in addition to photographs of well-known buildings and structures in Paris, there are everyday images of busy traffic, the Metro and a city centre park.

The accompanying teachers' notes offer a wide variety of ways to use the resources when teaching. There are additional suggestions for gathering visual information from the internet, as well as for developing resources from tourist materials. Opportunities to promote role-play are included in the activities to encourage understanding through empathy.

Photocopiable pages
The photocopiable pages in the book are also provided in PDF format on the CD-ROM and can be printed from there. They include:
▶ word cards containing essential vocabulary for the topics
▶ a mock-up of a passport
▶ a poem about a harbour
▶ a French dictionary of words relating to a café
▶ recipes for French snack meals.

Geography skills
The activities included in this chapter encourage the children to develop a variety of skills essential to geographical enquiry, such as recognising environmental features both physical and human, locating features and places, observing, questioning, describing and explaining what they can see. Speaking and listening skills form an important part of every activity and the activities include a very simple introduction to some French language. The ideas also focus on developing empathy with people visiting and living in another country: tourists travelling to and eating out in France and commuters travelling by road or Metro in Paris.

GOING TO FRANCE

NOTES ON THE CD-ROM RESOURCES

Map of cross-channel routes

France is the nearest mainland European country to Great Britain, with the width of the English Channel between Dover and Calais being around 35km. There are now several options for travelling across the channel, from ferries to Seacats (fast small vehicle ferries) as well as the Channel Tunnel. To travel through the tunnel, people can either take the Eurostar from London to Paris or the Eurotunnel from Folkestone, if they want to take a car. Heavy goods vehicles either take the Eurotunnel or ferries to transport goods to and from the European mainland.

This map shows the available routes between the south coast of England and France. It highlights how the four main sea areas form a continuous stretch of water around the British Isles. It would also be useful to have a general map on a smaller scale to hand, showing the relationship of the UK to Europe as a whole.

Discussing the map

▶ Review the children's ability to recognise the map of their own country. Give them the opportunity to find the British Isles on a smaller-scale map of Europe and on a large globe.
▶ Draw attention to and discuss the labels on the map.
▶ Discuss the idea that Great Britain and Ireland are *islands* while France is joined to other countries in the European *mainland*.
▶ Explain that if we want to go to France or other countries in mainland Europe we have to cross the sea. Show the children the English Channel and name it.
▶ Show the children that the map has a *key* and explain this simply. Use the key to draw attention to the ferry routes and count them together. Draw their attention to the channel tunnel route and explain what this is.

Activities

▶ Print out, enlarge and copy the map onto card. Ask the children to colour the countries and the sea. Cut out the pieces to make a puzzle to develop the children's understanding of the map.
▶ Organise a class or school-wide survey to find out how many people have been to France and how they travelled there. Help the children to plot the results on a bar chart.
▶ Cut out and laminate a collection of different kinds of ferry transport from travel brochures. Make an enlarged plan of the channel routes and display the ferries on appropriate journeys.

CROSSING THE ENGLISH CHANNEL

Dover marina, Seacat ferry

These photographs show Dover marina and a Hoverspeed Seacat ferry as it leaves Dover. Many ferries leave from Dover and the marina is also used by private boat owners.

The Seacat ferry takes about 650 passengers and can carry up to 140 vehicles. It takes 50 minutes to make the crossing on a Seacat ferry, but about two hours on a normal ferry boat. Passengers spend the journey comfortably in a well-serviced lounge with buffet facilities, or in good weather they can sit or stand on the rear deck.

Discussing the photographs

▶ Give the children some time to look at the photograph of the marina. Ask them what they can see, what kind of place they think it is and what it is for.
▶ Point out the piers and lighthouse and explain what these are for.
▶ Introduce the idea of going to France on a ferry and show the Seacat ferry picture.
▶ Ask the children what they think it would be like on the ferry. What kind of things might people need on the journey?
▶ Tell the children about time differences between the UK and Europe and the need to turn the clocks and watches forward one hour to European time.

Activities
▶ Use photocopiable page 20 to introduce the idea of needing passports in order to go to another country, and boarding cards to get onto ferries.
▶ Look at the official website of Dover Harbour Board (www.doverport.co.uk) to find out more about the Port of Dover, such as which ferries sail from there and what kind of attractions can be found at Dover marina.
▶ Talk about the sequence of a ferry journey from boarding to setting sail and then disembarking. Make a simple collage map of the English Channel and encourage imaginative role-play about a ferry crossing, using model (or cut out) cars and ferries.

Leaving England

The impressive white cliffs of Dover are symbolic of England. The cliffs are composed of chalk, which is a soft, easily eroded rock, and they vary in height, with the hilltops and valleys along the coast. This wavy line of white can be seen from across the channel on a clear day.

Dover Castle has historically watched over the harbour area from a good vantage point high on the cliff top whilst the highest point of the cliffs is the site of modern radar equipment, which monitors channel shipping – ensuring the safety of the ferries, especially in misty weather.

During the Second World War lookout bunkers were hollowed out of the soft chalk rock of the cliffs. These can be visited from the National Trust White Cliffs Experience centre whose website offers more information and images on www.nationaltrust.org.uk.

Discussing the photographs
▶ Tell the children that this is the view from the ferry as it leaves Dover for Calais. Ask the children to describe what they see.
▶ Explain that the wake of the Seacat is white because the powerful engines and propellers are churning up the water to make the boat go forward.
▶ Discuss the background of the photograph and talk about the cliffs and the castle.

Activities
▶ Play a recording of the song 'White Cliffs of Dover'. Explain why it is famous and teach the children the chorus.
▶ Draw a simple section of the channel showing the high cliffs, Dover Castle, the lighthouse, a long stretch of water and France. Laminate pictures of ferries and place them on the water with some 'travelling' in each direction. Let the children play 'ferry crossings', using the picture as a game board.

Port of Calais

Calais is the hub of the cross-channel commercial traffic due to its easy access to the French motorway network. The large dock area is always busy loading and unloading ferries and container ships. The Seacat travels through the main dock area on its way to the Hoverspeed terminal. Here the 'Calais 7' terminal can be seen with Sealink and P&O ferries loading. Smoke from the funnels of the P&O ferry indicates that it is nearly time to sail.

Discussing the photographs
▶ Explain to the children that this photograph is taken from the viewing deck as the Seacat arrives in France. What can the children see? Discuss safety and draw the children's attention to the lifebelt. Do the children know what it is for and why it is a bright orange colour?
▶ Introduce the word *docks* to the children. Ask them what they think happens there.
▶ Talk about the large ferries in more detail, explaining that the cars, lorries, caravans, buses and tankers can all travel on these big ferries. Explain that large doors open to let the vehicles drive on board.

Activities
▶ Make a large, simplified outline drawing of a ferry showing the interior with car decks on several levels. Make several copies and give each group of children a copy. Provide some suitably sized pieces of paper and ask the children to draw, colour and cut out a range of vehicles to stick onto the ferry car decks.

A SMALL FRENCH PORT: HONFLEUR

Pont de Normandie

Normandy is one of the most popular regions of France for British tourists to visit. It has a good coastline including extensive beaches and many old and picturesque settlements – one of which is the port of Honfleur, near the mouth of the River Seine. Honfleur can be approached easily from the channel ports of Le Havre and Dieppe and this journey now includes transit of one of the most spectacular new bridges in France – the Pont de Normandie (Bridge of Normandy).

This cable-stayed bridge, which was opened in 1995, has an overall length of 2km. It has dramatically improved local transport links between Normandy and the ports of Dieppe and Le Havre and has itself become a major tourist attraction.

Discussing the photograph
▶ Introduce the term *bridge* and explain this to the children. Tell them that this bridge is called the Pont de Normandie and that *pont* is the French word for bridge.
▶ Can the children guess why the middle of the bridge needs to be curved so high? Explain that the River Seine is used by large ships and barges that need to pass under the bridge.
▶ Use a flexible metre rule to demonstrate the curved shape of the bridge and explain that the Pont de Normandie is as long as 2000 metre rules. Think of a landmark that is two kilometres from your school and explain that this bridge would reach all the way from your school to this landmark.

Activities
▶ With the children's help, make a table of bridges in your locality. Use headings such as 'Name of bridge'; 'What does it cross?' and 'Why is it useful?'.
▶ Challenge the children to make bridges from construction kits or junk materials that will either support a toy vehicle in the centre without collapsing or allow a toy vehicle to pass underneath.
▶ Ask the children to collect pictures of bridges and sort these according to type.

Honfleur harbour

Honfleur is a small picturesque French port on the Normandie coast. It is a favourite place for tourists, sailing enthusiasts and artists who can be seen painting pictures of the boats and buildings reflected in the harbour. The harbour is surrounded by tall French houses, many of them hotels with restaurants or souvenir shops on the ground floor. It is protected from the open sea by strong harbour walls and is accessed via a lifting bridge at the seaward end.

Discussing the photograph
▶ Give the children plenty of time to look at the photograph in detail. Ask them to tell you what they can see.
▶ Ask the children what the weather is like. How do they know this?
▶ Explain that a harbour is a place that has been built to keep the boats safe – like a 'parking area' for boats. People may come here for a holiday and live on their boats.
▶ Read the Wes Magee poem 'The Harbour Wall' (photocopiable page 21), which will help the children to understand the function of a harbour.

Activities
▶ Ask the children to make a range of small boats from junk materials and provide a harbour model where their boats can be moored.
▶ Make a collage map of the class harbour. Encourage the children to recognise and describe the positions of their boats in the harbour, locating them on their collage map.

Eating out in Honfleur

This photograph shows some outdoor eating places in Honfleur. As in this country, cafés with outdoor seating are popular in sunny weather.

Discussing the photograph
▶ Encourage the children to talk about what the people in the photograph are wearing and what they are doing.
▶ Encourage the children to share experiences of eating outdoors in a café or restaurant.
▶ Talk about the buildings in the photograph. Are they like the buildings where we live? What is different and why?

Activities
▶ Set up a French café in the role-play area and encourage the children to role-play the parts of waiters and customers, using the French dictionary provided on photocopiable page 22. Provide pretend euros for payment.
▶ Encourage the children to write their own simple menus and price lists to use in the restaurant.
▶ Provide examples of French foods to try, such as baguettes, crêpes and croissants. Alternatively, make some typical French snacks with the children, using the recipes on photocopiable pages 23 and 24.

At the greengrocer's

Fruit and vegetables are popular in France, where a healthier diet that is less dependent on pre-cooked and processed foods is the norm. Vegetables and fruit are usually more locally-grown and fresher than in the UK, resulting in less long-distance haulage, and contributing to quieter roads. There is more attention to quality in terms of flavour than appearance. In short, their system is both healthier and more environmentally sustainable than ours.

This colourful outdoor fruit stall is part of a small fresh foods shop which also sells milk, cheese and some convenience goods. It offers a good opportunity for young children to consider similarities and differences between France and our country in an everyday context with which they can easily identify.

Discussing the photograph
▶ Ask the children what kind of shop this is and what it sells. Explain that all the fruits on display can be grown in France.
▶ Ask the children to tell you about fruits they like and dislike as well as fruits they have never tasted. Ask them to explain their reasons.
▶ Look at the way the fruits and vegetables are stored (slatted boxes and baskets). Explain that these containers are designed to allow the air to circulate. Talk about the process of ripening and keeping fruit fresh.

Activities
▶ Have an adult work with small groups of children to wash and prepare some fruit for tasting. Make record sheets for the children to complete, recording the names of the fruits, what they looked like and the children's preferences.
▶ Look at the labels on different European fruits. Make a note of where the fruits came from and find the places on a map.
▶ Make a class survey of favourite fruits. Total the results and display them in a bar graph.

THE BAYEUX TAPESTRY

Bayeux tapestry: Leaving France, Crossing the Channel, Landing at Pevensey

Bayeux is a small town in Normandy that can be easily accessed from Honfleur. Here, in an impressive exhibition centre, the magnificent Bayeux Tapestry (strictly speaking an embroidery), which is approximately 50cm tall and 70m long, is displayed. It tells the story of the events leading up to the Battle of Hastings (14 October 1066), the battle itself, and the conquest of England by the Normans led by William the Conqueror. The opportunity is provided here to explore the link between the UK and Normandy, to establish the significance of the word 'Norman' and to help children understand the significance of the English Channel and how the ways of crossing it have changed over the centuries.

The entire tapestry can be viewed on www.hastings1066.com/baythumb.shtml.

Discussing the pictures
▶ Show the pictures of the Norman ships crossing the channel and explain that in the days before books, people sometimes made pictures to tell a story. This picture was stitched on cloth. Show a real tapestry or an embroidered picture to consolidate the idea.
▶ Explain that these parts of the Bayeux tapestry show the Normans crossing the English Channel. The words on the picture: 'MARE TRANSIVIT ET VENIT AD PEVENESAE' are in Latin and they mean 'He crossed the sea and came to Pevensey'.
▶ Show the children where Pevensey and Hastings are on a map of the UK.
▶ Ask the children what they notice about the ships and the people in them. Discuss how these are similar and different to the ways we can cross the channel today.
▶ Consider how the boats in the picture must have moved. What would have happened to the boats in bad weather?

Activities
▶ Make a table during your class discussion to show the differences between crossing the channel in the time of the Norman invasions and today. Headings could be split under 2005 and 1066 and include: Why do/did people cross the Channel? What do/did people wear? What do/did people travel in? What do/did people take with them? How long is/was the journey?
▶ Provide a long length of linen-effect wallpaper. Help the children to gradually build up a long picture from cut-out images (a Hoverspeed boat, a lighthouse, sights in Paris and so on) to record the things they have learned about going to France.
▶ Encourage the children to write brief captions (including appropriate French words) to accompany their pictures and place these along the length of your class 'tapestry'.

A VISIT TO THE CAPITAL CITY: PARIS

Journey to Paris

Paris, the capital of France – and its most extensive conurbation, offers a great contrast to the small port of Honfleur. Both settlements, however, have links with the River Seine and it is possible to travel between them by river as well as road. This simple map shows the route from Honfleur to Paris.

Discussing the map
▶ Tell the children that, as part of their visit to France, you are going to take a trip to Paris, the capital city. Ask the children if they know what their capital city is and where it is.
▶ Explain that the red line is the road to Paris and the blue line is the River Seine.
▶ What do the children notice about the two lines? Why do they follow a similar route?

Activities
▶ Using the scale bar and a piece of string, work out the length of the journey with the children.
▶ Work out the distance from the children's own locality to their capital city. Is it more or less than the trip from Honfleur to Paris?

TRAVELLING IN PARIS

Video: the Arc de Triomphe

In this section the children are challenged to discuss the issues of congestion and air pollution and to begin to consider some alternative ways to travel in a large city.

Travelling by car is not the best way to explore Paris and there are other ways of travelling around the city. This video highlights the busy roads in Paris, as well as the hazards of crossing such a busy road.

The Arc de Triomphe, built by Napoleon I in the early 19th century to commemorate his war victories, is one of the most famous monuments in Paris. It contains a museum and a roof terrace from which there are wonderful views of the city. It stands on Place Charles de Gaulle – a huge traffic roundabout, known locally as L'Etoile, meaning 'the star. Twelve roads converge at this point – hence the traffic congestion! The Arc de Triomphe can be safely accessed via an underpass from the north side of the Avenues des Champs Elysées.

Discussing the video clip
▶ Show the clip to the children and tell them about the Arc de Triomphe. Explain why people want to go there to see it.
▶ Put the children in role as the pedestrians in the clip and ask them what they can see, hear and smell and how they feel about the busy traffic. Explain basic ideas about air pollution from motor vehicles.
▶ Can the children think of ways to make movement safer for pedestrians? Introduce and define the word *subway*.

Activities
▶ Ask different groups to look for a particular type of vehicle and try to count how many cars, coaches and so on they can see. Discuss the difficulties of this. Allow the children, working in pairs, to operate the video clip via the horizontal slide on the computer – this will enable them to see it in slow motion and they can stop it to count the categories of vehicles more accurately.
▶ Use the children's results to make a simple pictorial bar chart called 'Ten seconds of traffic in Paris'. Let the children make a comparison by counting ten seconds of traffic passing your school or at a nearby road junction.
▶ Make a list of the ways people are helped to cross the road in your local area and challenge the children to find ways of making it safer.

The Paris Metro

Like many large cities, Paris has an extensive underground Metro system. 'Metro' is short for 'le Metropolitain' and since it was first opened in 1891 it has grown to include 15 underground lines and 368 stations, 87 of which are junctions. It carries six million passengers per day and is usually the best way to travel around the city, for both local people and tourists. No building in Paris is more than 500 metres from a Metro station. The Metro is integrated with the RER (Réseau Express Régionale – the train system in and around Paris) and bus systems so that any part of the suburbs as well as all the railway stations and airports can be reached easily by public transport.

Tickets are usually bought as day passes or in little books called carnets to save time queuing. More information about the Paris Metro may be gained by consulting the website www.paris.org/Metro.

Discussing the photograph
▶ Ask the children to look carefully at the train and describe it. Explain that it is a Metro train in Paris and that it is in an underground station.
▶ Ask the children to think of ways that people could get underground to the trains (lifts, escalators and stairs). What are the advantages and disadvantages of each mode?
▶ Establish that some of the people on the platform are tourists and some are going to work.

Activities
▶ Invite the children to make a model to show how an underground railway works, using boxes and cardboard tubes. Challenge them to include 'escalators' made from concertina card and a 'lift' with pulleys.
▶ Challenge the children to find out where we have underground systems in our country and find maps of these. If there is an underground system in your locality, take the children for a visit.

GOING TO FRANCE

SIGHTSEEING IN PARIS

Walking in Paris

It is possible to see many of the sights on foot in Paris. There are footpaths along the River Seine where you can look at stalls selling paintings, books and souvenirs on the pavements. Tourist boats such as the well-known Bateaux Mouches offer excursions on the river, which link some of the important sights of the city.

Discussing the photograph
▶ Tell the children that this picture is taken on a walk in Paris.
▶ Ask the children to describe the features of the river and those on the banks of the river.
▶ Focus attention on the far side of the river. What is on the other side of the river? Why are trees planted there? Discuss the value of trees for shade and pollution reduction in urban areas.
▶ Talk about the people in the picture. What are they doing? Where might they be going? What can they hear? How do they feel about this place?

Activities
▶ Support the children in finding more images of the River Seine from tourist brochures or prepare a selection of photos on disk for them to view. A search on Google (images button) will bring up several photographs of Paris (some are copyright images).
▶ Ask the children to choose a favourite picture and say why they would like to visit this place.
▶ Let the children make a postcard to send to a friend showing something they have 'seen' in Paris.

Notre Dame Cathedral

The Notre Dame Cathedral was completed in 1330 (construction began in 1163). It is on the Ile de la Cité, an island in the centre of Paris, and is situated along the River Seine. During the French Revolution at the end of the 18th century, many of the cathedral's treasures were destroyed or plundered and the building was used as a warehouse. Between 1845 and 1868, the cathedral was restored, and a spire was built. It is still undergoing a general restoration programme to maintain its grand interior and exterior.

The cathedral is a classic example of Gothic architecture and one of its most well-known features is the gargoyles. It also served as the inspiration for Victor Hugo's *The Hunchback of Notre Dame* (originally entitled 'Notre Dame de Paris').

Discussing the photograph
▶ Tell the children that this huge Christian church is very important in Paris. It is called Notre Dame Cathedral, which means 'the cathedral of Our Lady'. Explain to the children that 'Our Lady' is Mary, the mother of Jesus.
▶ Ask the children to talk about the features of the building, introducing appropriate vocabulary such as *stone, tower, spire, stained-glass window* and so on. Encourage them to compare this with other churches or cathedrals in your local area.
▶ Encourage children from other cultures to talk about important buildings in their faith and how they are similar to or different from Notre Dame. Have appropriate pictures available for comparison.
▶ Tell the children that the cathedral is built on an island in the river so that the water goes round it on both sides. This was to help keep the cathedral safe from enemies. Nowadays you can cross bridges to visit the cathedral. Point out the strong walls that keep the building safe from the river today.

Activities
▶ Help the children to make a simple collage map or model (for example in a sand tray) to demonstrate the idea of a defensive site on an island in the river.
▶ Let the children design stained-glass windows for a cathedral like Notre Dame.
▶ Take the children on a visit to a cathedral near you to help them to appreciate the size and scale of such buildings.

Sacré Coeur Basilica

The Sacré Coeur (Sacred Heart) Basilica also occupies an imposing position, this time on the summit of a steep hill, in the district of Montmartre. The building was completed in 1914 and consecrated in 1919 after World War One and is popular with tourists on account of its beauty and the extensive views it affords of the city. There are 235 steps up to the cathedral. Close to the cathedral, and equally popular with visitors, is a small square populated by portrait artists.

Discussing the photograph
▶ Give the children time to look carefully at the photograph and ask if there are any clues which tell us what kind of a building this is. Draw attention to the domes, window shapes, decoration and statues.
▶ Invite the children to compare the basilica with Notre Dame to develop new vocabulary.
▶ What do the children think the tourists will be able to see as they look down on Paris.

Activities
▶ Challenge the children to design a new and impressive building to be built in the 21st century. Give them a brief which asks where they would build it, what materials they would use and what it would be used for.
▶ Tell the children about the portrait painters in Montmartre, showing them pictures from websites or brochures. Invite them to role-play as artists and subjects, painting portraits of each other. Display these around the classroom with prices in euros.

The Eiffel Tower

The Eiffel Tower – named after Gustav Eiffel, the contractor who designed and built it – is not only the most famous sight in Paris, but also the world's most visited and well-known structure. It was completed in 1889 for the World Fair, and commemorated the centenary of the French Revolution. It took over two years to build. It has had over 220 million visitors since then. There are 1665 steps to reach the top but most visitors ascend and descend by lift.

Discussing the photograph
▶ Show the children the photograph of the Eiffel Tower. Do they know the name of this structure?
▶ Tell the children about the tower, why it is there and why visitors from all over the world like to go up it.
▶ Make a list of other things in Paris that the children think may be visible from the top of the tower.

Activities
▶ Make posters advertising the best sights in Paris, giving reasons as to why they are good places to visit.
▶ Use a variety of construction equipment or junk materials to build a tower that resembles the Eiffel Tower.

Tuileries Gardens

The Tuileries Gardens (Jardin des Tuileries) began as an environmental reclamation experiment in the design of public gardens on the site of an old tile works and is now a popular venue for both Parisian families and visitors to the city. The gardens link the site of the Louvre museum to the Place de la Concorde and it is an important green space offering fresh air and peaceful space for recreation in the middle of a busy capital city. There are many forms of entertainment including a carousel, a park and adventure playground, a pond where model boats can be hired and sailed (as shown in the photograph), ice-cream sellers, cafés and open spaces to run around in.

Discussing the photograph
▶ Make a list of the activities the children can recognise under two headings – 'Adults' and 'Children'.

- Help the children to think about why it is important to have clean, peaceful spaces in the middle of a busy city.
- Ask the children to name and describe places like this that they have visited in their local area or while on holiday. What did they do there?

Activities
- Draw the children's attention to a derelict or neglected space in your locality or school grounds. Take them outside to map or photograph the area and discuss what could be improved there.
- Ask them to work in groups and think about what would make this place a better place to play. Ask them to design and map the proposed improvement, presenting their ideas to the rest of the class.

Eurostar

The Eurostar train service operates between three capital cities – London, Paris and Brussels, via the Channel Tunnel. Each train has 18 cars with a total passenger capacity of 770 people. The train's maximum speed is 300 kilometres per hour and it can complete the journey from London to Paris in 2 hours and 35 minutes. There are two catering carriages and a trolley snack bar on board as well as special areas where children can play. There are special facilities for disabled passengers. All staff on the train speak fluent English. More information about Eurostar and Eurotunnel is available on www.eurostar.com and www.eurotunnel.com.

Discussing the photograph
- Show the children the map of the Channel crossings that shows the Eurostar train route.
- Show the children the picture of the train. Discuss its size and design and how it travels.
- Consider the journey with the children. Discuss the similarities between countryside and city in the two countries and the differences between town and countryside that are common to both countries.

Activities
- Make a chart to show how long it takes to travel from London to Paris by Eurostar train, by ferry and car, and by aeroplane. Ask the children to write a short paragraph about which way they would like to travel and why.
- Help the children to complete the class dictionary of all the French words they have learned during their 'visit to France'.

NOTES ON THE PHOTOCOPIABLE PAGES

Word cards
PAGES 18–19

These cards contain some of the vocabulary for the children to learn and use when on a trip to France. They include:
- words to develop the children's geographical vocabulary
- words associated with France.

Read through the word cards with the children to familiarise them with the key words of the unit. Ask which words the children have heard before and clarify any they don't understand.

Activities
- Cut out and laminate the cards. Use them as much as possible when discussing the pictures and maps.
- Shuffle the cards and spread a set of cards on each group's table. Ask the children to find specific words as you call them out.
- Use the cards as a word bank to help the children to label pictures and to help them with longer pieces of writing. Encourage the children to add words to the bank.
- Use the word cards and the children's word bank to write captions for all the photographs.
- Begin a glossary with the words and include any other topic vocabulary used in the unit.

GOING TO FRANCE

Passport

PAGE 20

This activity introduces the idea of passports to the children. Explain that passports provide official photographic proof of identity. People need them in order to go on holiday abroad. On departure from this country the passport has to be shown to obtain a boarding card. On arrival in another country everyone has to show their passport to an official.

Activities
▶ Help the children to make their own passports containing a picture of themselves, their name and address, birth date and so on. Provide blank pages for the children to write and draw on, showing where they have been (during imaginary play).
▶ Role-play using the passports at a ferry terminal. Teach the 'passengers' to say *bonjour* and *merci* and the 'passport official' to say *Bienvenue à la France*.
▶ Create boarding cards to go with the passports. A boarding card is given at the ferry terminal, after the number of passengers, tickets and ID are checked.

'The harbour wall' poem

PAGE 21

This poem by Wes Magee describes how a harbour wall protects boats from rough winds. It explains quite a difficult concept in simple language and with accessible imagery.

Activities
▶ Use construction materials to make a harbour shape in a shallow water tray.
▶ Let the children make simple sailing boats using polystyrene or balsa wood for the hull, straws or twigs for the mast and a coloured paper for the sails. Group these in the harbour. Let the children test the effects of blowing wind on the boats and the water surface.
▶ Talk about safety in a harbour area for people as well as boats – lifejackets, lifebelts, lifeboats, luminous clothing and so on.
▶ Using the poem and the photograph 'Dover harbour' as stimuli, ask the children to make a picture map of a harbour. Give them a list of features to include – harbour walls, steps, ladders, lighthouses, flags and so on.

French dictionary

PAGE 22

Use this as a starting point to discuss the problem of language differences and how a dictionary can help us to overcome these.

Activities
▶ Enlarge the photocopiable page and show this to the children, covering up the translation. Ask them to read it (phonetically). Can they guess what the words mean?
▶ Ask the children if they can recognise any of the words. Encourage them to think about foreign words that are used in everyday language, such as *croissant*.
▶ Teach the children to say hello (*bonjour*); please (*s'il vous plait*); thank you (*merci*) and goodbye (*au revoir*) in French. Encourage the use of these words during role-play.

French recipes

PAGES 23–24

Try out these recipe ideas with the children to introduce them to French food. Encourage them to think of variations and to consider that it is not so different to food they may like to eat. *Croque-monsieur* is a simple savoury dish and is very popular in France. It is enjoyed as a snack meal rather like a Welsh rarebit or toasted sandwich. Ensure that you are aware of any food allergies in all activities that involve food.

Activities
▶ Make the crêpes and croque-monsieurs with the children and conduct a tasting exercise.
▶ Encourage the children to fill the crêpes with their own fillings and to test and score each other's creations.
▶ Ask the children to create their own menu board, in English or French, depending on their ability.

Going to France word cards

ferry
waves
train
cliffs
lighthouse
passport
boat
wall

Going to France word cards

busy

menu

waiter

snack

holiday maker

view

tower

cathedral

garden

Passport

GOING TO FRANCE

Where I've been

(Arrival / Departure stamps × 4)

My Passport

United Kingdom of Great Britain and Northern Ireland

picture of me

Passport number ....

Surname ....

First names ....

Nationality ....

Date of birth ....

Place of birth ....

Date of issue ....

'The harbour wall' poem

The harbour wall

In winter
when the wind blows wild
and the sea's as grey
as a muddy puddle,

the harbour wall
curls its long arm
around the boats
bobbing in a huddle.

'I'll keep you safe,'
the wall seems to say.
'Come here.' And it gives
the boats a cuddle.

Wes Magee

French dictionary

GOING TO FRANCE

baguette	french bread
bienvenue	welcome
boisson	drink
boule	scoop
bon appétit	enjoy your meal
café	coffee
chocolat	chocolate
citron	lemon
crêpe	pancake
eau	water
fraise	strawberry
fromage	cheese
glace	ice-cream
grand(e)	large, big
jambon	ham
lait	milk
petit(e)	small, little
salade	salad
soleil	sun
sucre	sugar

Numbers

1	un (une)		6	six
2	deux		7	sept
3	trois		8	huit
4	quatre		9	neuf
5	cinq		10	dix

French recipes (1)

Crêpes (French pancakes)

100g plain flour
10g melted butter
a pinch of salt
1 medium-sized egg
Approximately 250ml milk, or milk and water

To make the batter

- Sieve the flour and salt into a mixing bowl.
- Make a well in the centre and add the egg and a small quantity of the milk.
- Stir the mixture, gradually drawing in the flour and adding more milk as required, until a smooth batter with the consistency of thick cream is obtained.
- Add the melted butter and beat in the remaining liquid with a whisk until the mixture is like thin cream.
- Let it rest for half an hour.

To cook a crepe

- Heat a flat non-stick pan – wipe with melted butter or lard – pour in a small quantity of batter and tilt the pan to spread this over the base.
- Let it cook until the underside is golden brown.
- Loosen the edge with a spatula, then carefully turn or toss the pancake.

To serve

Transfer the pancake to a plate, add an appropriate sweet or savoury filling and serve.

French recipes (2)

GOING TO FRANCE

Croque-monsieur

- Grill a thick slice of bread on one side.
- Place toasted side down on the grill pan.
- Add a slice of cooked ham and a thick covering of hard cheese, preferably Gruyère, to the un-toasted side.
- Grill until the cheese is bubbling and turns golden brown.

Croque-madame

- Grill a thick slice of bread on one side.
- Place toasted side down on the grill pan.
- Add a slice of cooked ham and a thick covering of hard cheese, preferably Gruyère, to the un-toasted side.
- Grill until the cheese is bubbling and turns golden brown.
- Serve it topped with a fried egg.

Warning! This snack will be very hot, so eat it with a knife and fork to avoid burned fingers!

LIVING IN SCOTLAND

Content and skills

The 'Living in Scotland Gallery' on the CD-ROM found with this book, together with the teachers' notes and photocopiable pages in this chapter, provide a locality study that is appropriate for:
- ▶ 'A locality... in the United Kingdom... that has physical and/or human features that contrast with those in the locality of the school' (National Curriculum for England);
- ▶ 'a locality... elsewhere in the world which contrasts with that of the school' (National Curriculum for Wales);
- ▶ 'maintaining... a focus on the geography of Scotland' when studying people and place (National Curriculum for Scotland).

The study in this chapter enables children to begin to observe and describe the human and natural features of a new locality and to compare 'Living in Edinburgh' with their own local area.

After locating the country of Scotland and the capital city of Edinburgh, this chapter focuses initially on a small part of Edinburgh (a locality) and on Daisy and James who live there. It then moves further afield in the city and finally extends to a wider perspective of Scotland. This provides opportunities for additional small-scale studies and for further comparisons with the children's own experiences and local area.

To get the most from the study, encourage the children to compare their lives and experiences with Daisy's and James', identifying similarities as well as differences. Help them to think about what it is like to live in a city and the features that are found in a capital city.

You may use the resources sequentially or selectively – developing a locality study of Edinburgh, or looking at a particular human or natural feature (perhaps comparing it with a similar feature near the children's own school), providing local fieldwork opportunities in the process.

The activities in this chapter provide opportunities for geographical enquiry, using careful questioning based on the key question sequence from the National Curriculum as well as on your own and the children's questions. The sequence below relates to the National Curriculum level descriptions for assessment purposes:
- ▶ Where is the locality/place?
- ▶ What is it like?
- ▶ Why is it like this?
- ▶ How is it changing?
- ▶ How does it relate to/compare with other places?
- ▶ What is the environmental quality of the place like?
- ▶ How is it linked to other places in the world?

© Photodisc, Inc.

Resources on the CD-ROM

The resources on the CD-ROM provide a wide range of photographs from a variety of perspectives, including ground level, oblique and vertical aerial viewpoints, that introduce places and features in Scotland. There are pictorial and other maps as well as photographs. The pictorial resources can be printed out and used to compile a Big Book of 'Living in Scotland', including the children's own questions and comments.

Photocopiable pages

The emphasis on the photocopiable pages is pictorial, to make them inclusive and appropriate for most children in this age range. This means that the activities can provide formative assessment of children's geographical skills and understanding, rather than their literacy skills.

Geography skills

The focus of this chapter is on developing graphicacy skills – the essentially pictorial communication of spatial information – since a pictorial approach is inclusive and appropriate for most children of this age.

NOTES ON THE CD-ROM RESOURCES

Scotland in the British Isles

This map establishes the location of Scotland within the British Isles. The British Isles includes Great Britain and Ireland and all the islands around the coast; Great Britain is the largest island in the British Isles; and the United Kingdom is a country and includes England, Scotland, Wales, and Northern Ireland. The Republic of Ireland is a separate country.

Scotland was formerly a separate kingdom but was united with England in 1603 when James VI of Scotland also became James I of England, upon the death of Queen Elizabeth I.

Geographically, Scotland is the most northerly part of the UK, therefore the climate is colder and the winters longer and darker than further south. The landscape of Scotland has two distinct characteristics – the rolling hills of the Scottish Lowlands and the dramatic mountain scenery of the Highlands. The Scottish Highlands are the weathered remains of ancient mountain chains. Edinburgh is located in what is called the Midland Valley of Scotland.

Discussing the map
▶ Talk about the map, using the appropriate geographical vocabulary: land, sea, coast, mountains and so on.
▶ Talk about where it would be possible to get a view of Scotland like this – refer to a satellite, rather than a 'bird's-eye' view.
▶ Ask the children what a map is used for.
▶ Introduce Edinburgh as the capital city of Scotland.

Activities
▶ Show the children where Scotland is on a globe and in an atlas. Point out where the children's own locality is.
▶ Provide a variety of picture, road and world atlases for the children to explore. Help them to locate Scotland and Edinburgh. Show them how to use the index to find places.
▶ Use the map with photocopiable page 39 to help the children to focus on the location of Scotland and its capital.

EDINBURGH

Aerial view of Edinburgh

This photograph shows an oblique aerial view of Edinburgh from a plane approaching the city from the east. Leith Docks, Arthur's Seat and Salisbury Crags are visible, as is Edinburgh Castle (just) on the right, with the city centre in between.

Edinburgh is the capital city of Scotland, with a population of approximately 456,000. It is dominated by seven hills including the rocky volcanic hills of Castle Rock, with its imposing Edinburgh Castle, Arthur's Seat and Calton Hill. The volcanoes were active some 350 million years ago, and will not erupt again. The city is often called the 'Athens of the North' because of its classical architecture. The Old Town formed around Castle Rock and was enclosed within a city wall. The New Town, with its distinctive Georgian geometrical layout, was started in the late 18th century. Suburbs were the result of further expansion in the late 19th and early 20th centuries, with more recent development culminating in multi-storey flats. Edinburgh is an 'international' city, much visited by tourists, especially at the time of the Edinburgh festival.

Discussing the photograph
▶ Ask the children what they can see in the photograph.
▶ Talk about where the photograph was taken from.
▶ Ask the children if they have been in a plane. What could they see from the window?

Activities
▶ To help the children understand this perspective, use a clip from the 'Barnaby Bear Goes To Dublin' video (Barnaby Bear 1 Video Plus Pack, BBC Schools) showing his plane taking off from the airport and flying over land.

LIVING IN SCOTLAND

▶ Ask the children to imagine what their own school and locality would look like from a plane. Invite the children to draw a picture of what they think they would see.

Pictorial map of central Edinburgh

This is a pictorial map of the centre of Edinburgh, showing the Castle, Princes Street and Gardens and the Royal Mile, with Old Town (bottom/south, in the area enclosed by Lawnmarket, Grassmarket and George IV Bridge) and New Town (top/north, on the other side of Queen Street Gardens). It is a tourist map (published by James Brown Designs).

Discussing the map
▶ Explain that the map shows the city centre.
▶ Ask the children what they can see. Make a vocabulary list with their suggestions.
▶ Ask the children what a map would be used for. Tell them that this is a plan of the streets of central Edinburgh to help visitors find their way around the city.
▶ Help the children to identify the Edinburgh landmarks: Edinburgh Castle, Princes Street, Princes Street Gardens, the Royal Mile, Scott Monument.
▶ Talk about the features on the map: buildings, railway lines and station, gardens/parks, road patterns and the castle on a hill.
▶ Help the children to identify the similarities and differences between Edinburgh and the place they live in.

Activities
▶ Use boxes or large building blocks to build some streets like those in the map. Provide a (real or pretend) camera for the children to view the model from different levels, from the side, at an angle and from above, and talk about what they see from different positions. Ask them where they think the map-maker was looking from.
▶ Encourage the children to make a toy camera with a viewfinder to use with the activities.
▶ Ask the children to make a LEGO model castle and place it on an up-turned bucket to represent the volcanic hill.
▶ Ask the children to use their 'camera' and draw the 'photograph' taken from different viewpoints: eye-level, an oblique angle and from above. This will help them towards an understanding of plan view.
▶ Use the map to ask children how they would get from one place to another in Edinburgh. Encourage the use of directional language such as 'left', 'right' and 'straight ahead'.

DAISY AND JAMES

Daisy and James' local area

This is James and Daisy, walking along Royal Crescent on their way home from school. James is nearly four years old and his sister Daisy is five years old. They live in a flat in Royal Crescent on the northern edge of the Georgian New Town in Edinburgh.

Daisy goes to primary school and James goes to nursery. Daisy likes playing with dolls, dressing-up and going to ballet and swimming lessons. She is also beginning to learn tennis. James likes playing with his toy animals, especially elephants. He is fascinated by foreign languages and is learning French at nursery. Daisy and James both like to draw and colour, and to have bedtime stories read to them. Since their grandparents live in Fife, Scotland and Devon, England, and Daisy's godmother lives in Kenya, they are both seasoned travellers.

Discussing the photograph
▶ Ask the children what they can see, and make a vocabulary list for the photograph.
▶ Explain that this photograph shows two children, Daisy and James, and a road in the city of Edinburgh, where they live.
▶ Talk about what the children think it might feel and sound like in Royal Crescent.

Activities
▶ Use a website such as www.multimap.com (enter EH3 6PZ) to find Royal Crescent on a street map, changing scale as appropriate. Ask the children where they think Daisy and

LIVING IN SCOTLAND

James are walking to. Use the aerial photograph facility to view an aerial perspective, and 'roam' southwards to reach the area covered by the pictorial map.
▶ Cover and paint cereal boxes to make a street like Royal Crescent; repeat the activity for a road near school. View it from different angles such as oblique and vertical aerial views.
▶ Suggest that more able children draw their model street from above, moving towards making a pictorial map.

Daisy going to school

This photograph shows Daisy walking to school with her father. Her school has 12 classes. There is a hard playground, where she plays before school starts, but no school field.

Discussing the photograph
▶ Ask the children what they can see and make a vocabulary list for the photograph. Can the children provide a title for the picture?
▶ How do the children get to school? Discuss road safety and the use of the crossing attendant.
▶ Talk about the Royal Mail van and other vehicles in the photograph.

Activities
▶ Compare the children's own school with Daisy's.
▶ For fieldwork study, walk around the outside of your school with the children. Encourage them to take digital photographs of the school and its surroundings. Use appropriate geographical vocabulary to describe the building and the children's position in relation to it (such as *near*, *next to*, *outside* and so on).

James at nursery, James at lunchtime

These two photographs show James at his nursery. In the first photograph, he is in the playground. He is sliding down the slide as Daisy arrives to meet him. In the second, James is eating his lunch at nursery. This kind of setting will still be familiar to younger children.

Discussing the photographs
▶ Ask the children what they can see and make a vocabulary list for each photograph. What titles would the children give the photographs?
▶ Develop positional language by asking the children to describe the things they might do in the playground (such as *go up/down the steps*, *down the slide*, *on the bikes* and so on).
▶ Talk about what James is having for lunch (pasta, peas, drink). What do the children like to eat and drink for their lunch? Use this as an opportunity to talk about a healthy diet.
▶ Talk about seasonal food and the long distances much of our food travels to reach our shops and markets.

Activities
▶ Ask the children what they would like to ask Daisy or James about their home, school and street. What would the children like to tell Daisy and James about their own environment?
▶ Ask the children to identify the similarities and some differences between their lives and Daisy's and James'.
▶ Where do the children like to play (inside and outside) in their own school? Invite them to design indoor and outdoor play areas.

IN AND AROUND EDINBURGH

Shopping on the Royal Mile

Daisy is looking in a shop window in the Royal Mile (High Street) in Old Town. The shop is at the very edge of the pictorial map. The Royal Mile, which goes from Edinburgh Castle to the Palace of Holyroodhouse, in Edinburgh Old Town, is a tourist attraction. This shop displays what is perceived as traditional Scottish costume (a tartan kilt with all the accessories) as well as other tourist goods.

LIVING IN SCOTLAND

Discussing the photograph
▶ Ask the children where Daisy is. What is she doing? What else can the children see? What is reflected in the window? Make a word list together.
▶ Talk about the clothes on display – the kilt, tartan, shirt and jacket or waistcoat. Link this with the picture of Highland dancers (see below).

Activities
▶ Locate the Royal Mile on the pictorial map and look in detail at the buildings on the right of the picture, noticing the shops and the uses for the floors above.
▶ For fieldwork study, walk around some local shops looking high as well as at ground level to see the uses of the different floors. Record with a digital camera.
▶ Visit websites such as www.houseoftartan.co.uk or www.geo.ed.ac.uk/home/scotland/dress.html to find out about tartan. Find tartans for specific clan names or design your own.

James at Edinburgh Zoo, Zebra

Edinburgh Zoo is on a hillside on Corstorphine Road, three miles west of the city centre. The zoo is owned by The Royal Zoological Society of Scotland, which was founded in March 1909. The Zoo opened in July 1913. It is now one of Europe's leading centres of conservation, education and research.

The plan of the zoo clearly shows routeways and has good symbols to indicate the location of the different animals and birds – James was truly fascinated by it.

Discussing the photographs
▶ Ask the children what a plan is. What does the plan of the zoo show?
▶ Look at the use of symbols, rather than words, to show where the animals are. Why do the children think symbols are used instead of words?
▶ James saw lots of animals and birds at the zoo, including sea lions being fed, penguins and zebras. Talk about where all these animals live naturally. What would they eat there? How does being in the zoo differ?

Activities
▶ Point out the pattern of the zebra. Why do the children think the zebra's pattern is good for a crossing?
▶ Ask the children to talk about their own experiences of zoos. Ask them to name some zoo animals and then locate the animals' country of origin in an atlas.
▶ For fieldwork, visit a nearby animal collection, farm or zoo. Talk about the animals' food, habits, and where they come from. Help the children to find out about their favourite animal and make a page for a Big Book about it.
▶ Encourage the children to invent symbols for different parts of their school. Place these on a plan of the school. If this is too challenging, create some symbols yourself and ask the children where they should go. Let the children navigate you round the school to put the symbols up in the appropriate places.

Map of the Royal Botanic Gardens

The Royal Botanic Garden Edinburgh was founded in the 17th century as a 'Physic Garden', growing medicinal plants. It now has four sites (Edinburgh, Argyll, Galloway and Borders), and hosts the second richest collection of plant species in the world. The map shows a high-angle oblique pictorial plan of the gardens.

Discussing the map
▶ Look at the pictorial map and help the children to understand what it shows.
▶ Do the children think all the trees are the same? Talk about what trees look like at different times of the year.
▶ Ask the children whether there is a similar park or garden near to where they live.

Activities
▶ Using the map, work out a short route round the Garden and ask the children to imagine they are walking along it. Ask them to describe what they would be seeing and passing. Ask

them to imagine how tall the plants are, and what they smell and feel like. What sounds can they hear?
▶ Enter postcode EH3 5LR on the website www.multimap.com. Navigate around and work out the route that Daisy and James take from Royal Crescent (EH3 6PZ) to walk to the Garden's entrance in Arboretum Place. (Use 1:10,000 scale with the children and 1:25,000 yourself.)
▶ For fieldwork, visit the nearest suitable park, woods or gardens to experience different trees, shrubs and flowers. Ask the children to record a range of flora with a digital or film camera. Collect leaves, bark rubbings, seeds and so on. Feel, smell and listen to the environment. Do the children think that it is always like this there?
▶ Make a return visit to your chosen place. This time, provide a map with a route marked and ask the children to guide you along a pre-planned route. Ask adult helpers to draw or write on the map information given to the children including sights, sounds, smells and textures.

Princes Street: busy street, shop fronts

Princes Street is the main shopping street in the centre of the city of Edinburgh, paralleling George Street and Queen Street, part of the Georgian New Town (see the pictorial map). The first photograph shows a busy street scene, looking down Princes Street from the top of a double-decker bus, travelling eastwards. The bus was approaching St John's Church (extreme left of the pictorial map). Princes Gardens is on the right and Charlotte Street is the turning on the left.

The second photograph shows the ground level view of some shops situated in Princes Street.

Discussing the photographs
▶ Explain that Princes Street is the main shopping street in Edinburgh. Ask the children to compare it with the main shopping street where they live.
▶ Look at the skyline in 'Princes Street: busy street' and point out some of the different features:
– The Scott Memorial. *Are there any memorials or statues near your school/in your town?*
– The Balmoral Hotel clock tower. *Are there any hotels near your school? Have you stayed in a hotel? What was it like?*
– The 'Athenian acropolis' on Calton Hill (an unfinished monument started in 1816 replicating the Parthenon in Athens, as a memorial to the dead of the Napoleonic Wars).
▶ Ask the children if they know whether there is a war memorial in their town. Talk about the poppy wreaths that are laid at war memorials in November each year.
▶ Look at the busy street picture together and talk about the different ways that people are getting around.
▶ Look at the traffic. How many different types of transport are there? Which forms of transport do the children use?
▶ Look at the road signs, symbols and markings. What do they mean or indicate?
▶ Look at 'Princes Street: shop fronts'. What types of shops are shown? Are any familiar? Identify the tourist shop and the bus stop.
▶ Talk about the buildings' street-level and upper floors. What might they be used for?

Activities
▶ Use these photographs in conjunction with the pictorial map to help the children begin to understand the relationship between the different perspectives.
▶ Encourage the children to build a LEGO model of a city, or a few streets. Ask them to draw it from above, leading on to making a pictorial map of it. Alternatively use software, such as SEMERC's 'My Town' or similar.
▶ Use transport toys to make a model of a road like Princes Street. Role-play road safety situations.

Scottish National Portrait Gallery: outside, inside

The impressive Scottish National Portrait Gallery on Queen Street was built of Scottish red sandstone in 1885 to 1890. Statues of famous Scots decorate the facade. The portrait that James is looking at in the Gallery entrance hall is of John Richie Findlay (1824–98), sometime owner of *The Scotsman* newspaper, who founded the National Portrait Gallery of Scotland and donated its building to the nation (postcode EH2 1JD for www.multimap.com).

Discussing the photograph
▶ Talk about the meaning of the words *gallery*, *art gallery* and *portrait*. Discuss the ornate outside of the building.
▶ Ask the children if there are any similar ornate buildings close to where they live.
▶ What do the children think James will see inside? He sees portraits and sculptures (marble busts) of famous people connected with Scotland.

Activities
▶ Create your own portrait gallery by encouraging the children to paint portraits and make clay busts of each other. Alternatively, make a portrait gallery by painting or collecting pictures of famous people the children have heard of. Encourage the children to make beautiful frames for their portraits.
▶ Plan a visit to your nearest art gallery. Encourage the children to work out a route on an appropriate map. Collect a plan of the gallery to talk about the visit in school afterwards.

Edinburgh Castle

Edinburgh Castle is the best-known and most visited historic building in Scotland. It dominates the city from its position perched at the top of an extinct volcanic hill. The mixture of architecture reflects the castle's complex history. The oldest part, a tiny chapel, is Edinburgh's oldest building, dating from the 12th century. The sound of the One O'Clock Gun, fired at the castle, resounds over Edinburgh daily.

This photograph was taken from Princes Street, across Princes Gardens.

Discussing the photograph
▶ Talk about the position of the castle. Why is it a good position? Tell the children about its use for the Edinburgh Tattoo and about the One O'clock Gun.
▶ What time of year do the children think the photograph was taken? Talk about the autumn colours on some of the trees.
▶ Talk about the trees near to the school and the season you are currently in. Try to establish a year-long 'tree watch' of a few trees near your school, taking monthly photographs.

Activities
▶ Using the pictorial map and the photograph, ask the children to speculate about the view of Edinburgh they would get if they were looking over the castle wall. Ask them to explain their answer (this will assess their spatial understanding of the work so far).
▶ Make a collection of castle pictures and books and encourage the children to make models, paint pictures and draw plans of them. Collect names of castles and mark them on a map of the UK.
▶ Use large cardboard boxes or packing cases to construct a play castle in a suitable space.

SCOTLAND

The Forth rail bridge, The Forth road bridge

These two photographs show the road bridge and the rail bridge over the Firth of Forth, connecting Edinburgh to Fife and the north of Scotland.

The Forth rail bridge, which crosses the River Forth between South Queensferry and North Queensferry, is nine miles west of Edinburgh. It has been described as 'one of the most spectacular man-made landmarks in Scotland'. It was opened in 1890. It took seven years to build this solid cantilever bridge. It still carries the East Coast mainline railway one and a half miles over the Forth, north from Edinburgh to Fife, Dundee and Aberdeen.

The Forth road bridge took six years to build and was opened in 1964. At the time it was the longest suspension bridge in Europe. It replaced four vehicle ferries between South and North Queensferry that had made over 40,000 crossings a year, carrying 1.5 million people, 600,000 cars and 200,000 goods vehicles.

LIVING IN SCOTLAND

Discussing the photographs
▶ Show the two photographs to the children and tell them that these bridges provide two ways of crossing the Firth of Forth, which is a stretch of water close to Edinburgh.
▶ Discuss what goes over or on and what goes under each bridge. Ask the children to identify which bridge is which. How could they tell?
▶ What does the sign '30' mean? Talk about this speed limit and encourage explanations for it. (Roadworks have closed the left-hand carriageway.)

Activities
▶ Locate the Firth of Forth and the bridges on maps of Scotland.
▶ Use www.camvista.com/scotland/edinburgh/ and click on 'Forth Road Bridge' and 'Forth Rail Bridge' for a webcam showing a panoramic view. (This site includes other useful webcams of Edinburgh and elsewhere in Scotland.)
▶ Complete the worksheet.
▶ Look at pictures of other bridges and identify the rivers they cross. Talk about how Tower Bridge in London opens to let boats pass.

Winter sports at Aviemore

Aviemore is in the Cairngorm Mountains. It is a beautiful area with both forests and mountains, where green tourism is increasingly important, to sustain it for the enjoyment of future generations. The Cairngorm ski area began to be developed in the 1960s and is still being improved. It is the altitude of the mountains, with their snow cover, and their rounded, rather than jagged, shape that has encouraged skiing here.

Discussing the photograph
▶ Ask the children what time of the year they think it is and why. Notice that the snow is on the tops of the mountains and not in the warmer valleys.
▶ Ask the children if they have any experience of snow. Does it snow where they live? When does it snow? What do they do in the snow?
▶ What do the children think the people in the photograph are doing?
▶ Discuss the types of games and sports that can be played outdoors in winter.

Activities
▶ Collect some Winter Travel Brochures and make a Big Book about winter sports. Talk about the clothes we wear in winter and the special clothes that people wear for winter sports.
▶ Make a list of the countries that offer winter sports holidays and find them on a globe. Is there a pattern to the distribution of these places?
▶ Read the children the Raymond Briggs' story *The Snowman* (Picture Puffin) and visit the website www.thesnowman.co.uk/home.htm.

Urquhart Castle at Loch Ness, Tourist shop

'Loch' is the Scottish word for lake. Most lochs are long and thin, in steep-sided valleys. Loch Ness is, perhaps, the most famous because of the legend of the Loch Ness monster, or Nessie. The legend of the Loch Ness monster begins with ancient stone carvings of an unidentified aquatic animal. Adamnan recorded in AD 565 that St Columba saw the monster attack and kill a man swimming in the River Ness. The legend resurfaced in 1930 when three fishermen claimed that something that was about 6 metres long, spouting water into the air, made their boat rock violently. They were convinced it was a live creature. The tale reached the press and the legend was reborn and has been growing ever since, but still without sound evidence. For further details of the Nessie legend see www.crystalinks.com/loch_ness.html.

Urquhart Castle, now picturesque ruins, is on a rocky peninsula two miles from Drumnadrochit on the banks of Loch Ness. There was probably a fortification or look-out point there as early as the 6th century, but, after a chequered history, the building was blown up in 1692 to prevent it becoming a Jacobite stronghold.

Discussing the photographs
▶ Talk about what a Scottish loch is. Discuss how the water comes from rivers flowing into the loch and from rainfall and runoff from the hills and mountains around.

LIVING IN SCOTLAND

▶ Ask the children if they have heard of the Loch Ness monster. Introduce the legend. Do they believe it?
▶ Show them the second picture of the tourist shop. Where is James? What do they think he is buying? (A Nessie toy.)
▶ Discuss the idea of a 'souvenir'. Have the children ever bought any? If so, what and where?

Activities
▶ Encourage the children to imagine and to draw Nessie with the loch around 'her'. Challenge them to make a clay model based on their drawing.
▶ Make up a class story about the Loch Ness monster. Use the children's story and pictures to create a Big Book.
▶ Create a souvenir shop in the classroom selling Scottish things such as tartan, shortbread and oatcakes.
▶ Make a list of geographical terms for water: *lake*, *pond*, *river*, *stream*, *canal* and so on. Ask the children to collect pictures of these different types of water (perhaps from holiday brochures).

Dancing at the Highland Games

Highland games are popular in northern Scotland. They are usually a combination of Scottish sports (such as tossing the caber [a 6m-long tree trunk] and tug-o'-war) and customs (agriculture, Highland dancing and bagpipe competitions). This picture shows two girls performing a Highland dance.

Discussing the photograph
▶ Ask the children what they think the photograph shows. What kind of event is it? What are the people doing? Tell the children about the Highland Games.
▶ Talk about equivalent events that the children have experienced such as fairs, festivals, agricultural shows and so on.

Activities
▶ Encourage the children to draw a picture of themselves dancing or playing their favourite sport.
▶ Play a recording of some bagpipe music and encourage the children to try some Scottish dancing.

Scottish music: Catherine-Ann MacPhee

This song introduces the children to the idea that English is not the only language of the British Isles. Welsh children will, of course, already know this, but here they will meet another example. Although most people in the Scottish Highlands speak English, Gaelic is the traditional language, and similar languages are spoken in Ireland and the Isle of Man. Gaelic is still widely spoken in, for example, the Western Isles. Catherine-Ann MacPhee, who grew up on the Island of Barra, Outer Hebrides, sings beautiful Gaelic songs. These include 'Hì Ri Ri O Ra III Ó', a love song known throughout Gaelic Scotland and beyond.

Discussing the music
▶ Ask the children what they think the song is about. What sort of mind-pictures does it create?
▶ Talk about language in general. What languages do the children know about? Have any of the children heard different languages spoken when on holiday, for example?

Activities
▶ Introduce the children to other Scottish folk, dance or marching music, played on bagpipes, drums, accordion and fiddle. Also listen together to some music and folksongs in other languages and from other cultures.
▶ Label (geographical) pictures in different European and other languages.
▶ Invite speakers of other languages into the classroom and help the children to learn words and songs in other languages spoken by children in the class.

LIVING IN SCOTLAND

Hogmanay in Edinburgh

In Scotland, Hogmanay (New Year's Eve) is celebrated with great enthusiasm. In Edinburgh there is a huge street party in Princes Street and Gardens, with a fairground and fireworks.

Discussing the photograph
▶ Talk about what time of day it is and why there is a big celebration.
▶ Ask the children to describe what they see in the picture. Can they recognise any sights in Edinburgh? (Princes Street on the right, Edinburgh Castle on the left.)
▶ Ask the children what 'New Year' means. How do they celebrate New Year with their own families?

Activities
▶ Talk about fireworks and when we have them. Invite the children to make a wax-resist fireworks painting by making bright fireworks patterns with crayons and then washing over the patterns in dark paint.
▶ Use the opportunity to do some calendar work, looking at and counting the days of the week and months of the year starting with the first of January.

Highland cattle

The stereotypical images of the Scottish Highlands are mountains, heather and highland cattle. The reality is somewhat different – the mountains are spectacular but highland cattle can be very difficult to find in Scotland!

Discussing the photograph
▶ Ask the children what the landscape is like in the photograph. How does it compare to their own locality? Have the children ever been to a mountainous area?
▶ Talk about cattle and explore the children's knowledge of farm animals – why we keep them and what food and other products we get from them.
▶ Talk about scale (something young children find very difficult). Some children have no idea about the size of a cow, or other animals. It is useful to compare them with the size of different types of dog.

Activities
▶ Paint landscape pictures of mountains and the landscape near your school.
▶ Collect and make a scrapbook of farm animals, linked to the food and other products we get from them (treat this subject sensitively).
▶ Discuss a typical breakfast, lunch and/or dinner. Ask the children where each item comes from (which animal or plant rather than which country or shop – although this could be an extension activity).

Aberdeen docks

Daisy and James visit their cousins near Aberdeen. Aberdeen, 'the granite city' is an important sea port on the north-east coast of Scotland. The docks provide the shipping links with the North Sea oil rigs and gas fields as well as ferry services to Orkney and Shetland. This photograph shows a ship that goes to the oil rigs and there is a prominent helicopter pad on it. Helicopters are in constant contact with the rigs because, in times of emergency, it is the quickest way to rescue people. As well as commercial vessels, passenger ferries also sail from Aberdeen docks.

Discussing the photograph
▶ Explain to the children what a dock is. Point out the helicopter platform. Why do the children think it is there?
▶ Point out Leith docks in the 'Aerial view of Edinburgh' and tell the children that the ship in this photograph would be based in a similar place.
▶ Talk about the ships, about oil and about the other traffic. Discuss ferries and the journeys they make. Remind the children of the image of the Forth road bridge and how this replaced ferries across the Firth of Forth.

LIVING IN SCOTLAND

Activities
▶ Locate Aberdeen, St Andrews and Glasgow on a map. Talk about their position in relation to Edinburgh.
▶ Make models of boats and ships from a wide range of construction kits and other materials.
▶ Link the image of the ship with ideas of floating and sinking. Make boat shapes out of aluminium foil and polystyrene take-away food containers and load them to see how much 'cargo' they will take. Ask the children to describe what is happening and to record their work with drawings or digital photographs.

NOTES ON THE PHOTOCOPIABLE PAGES

Word cards   PAGES 36–38

These cards contain some of the vocabulary for the children to learn and use when looking at life in Scotland. They include:
▶ words to develop the children's geographical vocabulary
▶ words associated with Scotland and Edinburgh
▶ words relating to human and physical features.
Read through the word cards with the children to familiarise them with the key words of the unit. Ask which words the children have heard before and clarify any they don't understand.

Activities
▶ Cut out and laminate the cards. Use them as much as possible when discussing the pictures and maps.
▶ Shuffle the cards and spread a set of cards on each group's table. Ask the children to find specific words you call out.
▶ Use the cards as a word bank to help the children label pictures and to help them with longer pieces of writing. Encourage the children to add words to the bank.
▶ Use the word cards and the children's word bank to write captions for all the photographs.
▶ Begin a glossary with the words and include any other topic vocabulary used in the unit.

Map of the British Isles   PAGE 39

Use this blank map of the British Isles to reinforce the children's understanding of the parts that make up the United Kingdom as well as their capitals and flags.

Activities
▶ Add the children's own locality to the map. Ask them which part of the UK they live in. Which is the nearest capital city?
▶ Cut out the labels and ask the children to sort them into city and country.
▶ Ask the children to identify and label the capital cities and the parts of the UK.

Crossing the Firth of Forth   PAGE 40

This is a simplified drawing of the Forth rail and road bridges crossing the Firth of Forth where the River Forth flows into the North Sea. 'Firth' is the Scottish term for a long narrow estuary (wide part of a river near the sea). The Firth of Forth railway bridge was built in the Victorian times (completed in 1890).

Activities
▶ Explain what the Firth of Forth is.
▶ Ask the children to think about and list the different ways of crossing a stretch of water.
▶ Ask the children to draw forms of transport in the appropriate places.
▶ Use the labels to match the different forms of transport and features. Encourage the children to add more modes of transport to the picture.
▶ Design and build a model of the bridges to show the different ways of crossing the River Forth.

Scotland word cards

LIVING IN SCOTLAND

country
Edinburgh
Scotland
capital
city
town
map
place

Features word cards

LIVING IN SCOTLAND

coast
hill
land
landscape
mountains
river
habitat

Features word cards

buildings
zoo
castle
gardens
parks
road
station
street

Map of the British Isles

LIVING IN SCOTLAND

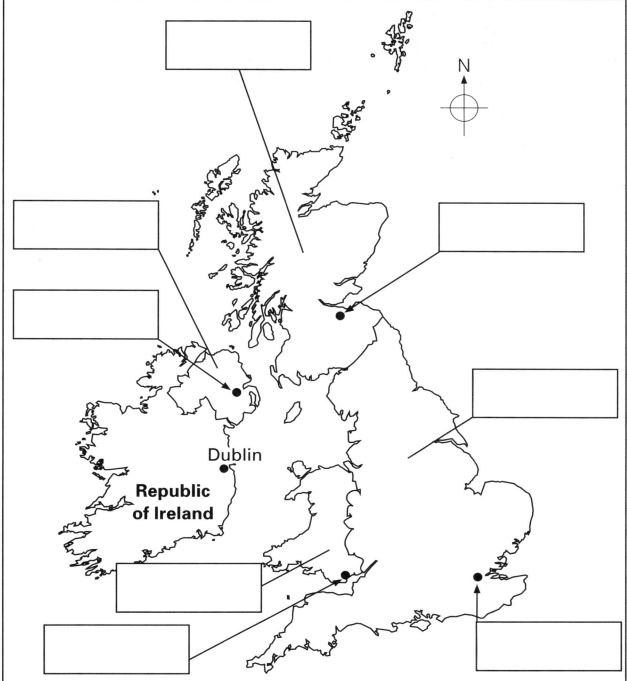

- Colour in Scotland on the map.

- Cut out these labels and match them to the correct places on the map.

Scotland	England	Wales	Northern Ireland
Edinburgh	London	Cardiff	Belfast

Crossing the Firth of Forth

LIVING IN SCOTLAND

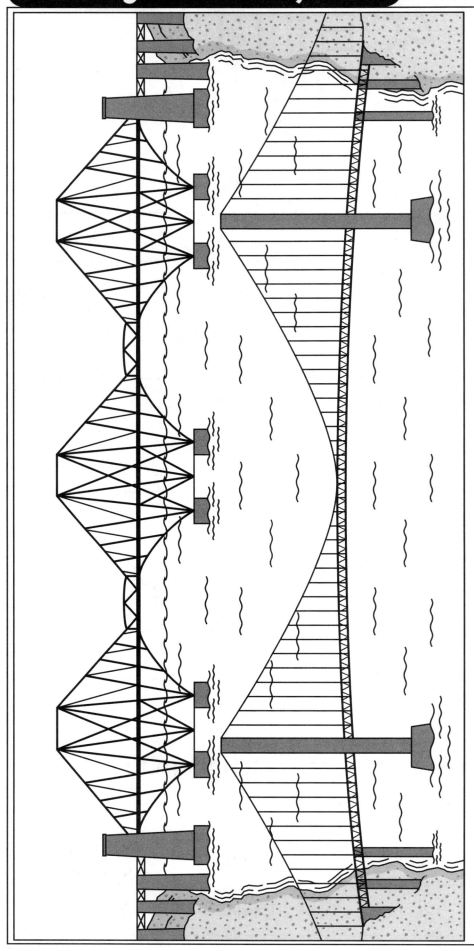

- On the picture, draw:

  1 train   2 boats   3 cars

- Cut out these labels and match them to the picture.

Forth road bridge	Forth rail bridge	Firth of Forth
boat	car	train	land

A VILLAGE IN THE GAMBIA

Content and skills
The Living in The Gambia Gallery on the CD-ROM, together with the teachers' notes and photocopiable pages in this chapter, provide a locality study that is appropriate for an overseas locality that contrasts with the children's own school and locality. It could also form the foundation for a Key Stage 2 study on 'a locality in a country that is less economically developed' (than the UK).

Lamin K Darboe's family is introduced and their compound located within Mandinari and The Gambia. Pictures illustrate their way of life, both in Mandinari and through their contacts with other places, including the town of Serekunda and the capital city of Banjul. Encourage the children to compare their lives and experiences with those of the Darboe family, especially the children. By focusing on the similarities between the two different ways of life the children will be helped to develop positive attitudes towards a very different, and economically poorer, way of life. The emphasis on family and community will show an emotional and social richness.

© Margaret Mackintosh

The resources linked to this chapter can be used sequentially (to develop a locality study of Mandinari), or selectively (using particular aspects to develop smaller studies, such as learning about food from production to consumption).

The activities in this chapter provide opportunities for geographical enquiry, using careful questioning based on the key question sequence from the National Curriculum, as well as on your own and the children's questions. The sequence below relates to the National Curriculum level descriptions for assessment purposes:
▶ Where is Mandinari?
▶ What is it like?
▶ Why is it like this?
▶ How is it changing?
▶ How does it relate to, or compare with, other places the children have studied?
▶ What is the environmental quality of Mandinari (and Serekunda and Banjul) like?
▶ How is it (Mandinari, Banjul, The Gambia) linked to other places in the world?

Resources on the CD-ROM
The resources on the CD-ROM provide a wide range of pictorial images from a variety of perspectives, including ground level and oblique aerial viewpoints. The photographs show Lamin Darboe's family and other people from Mandinari going about their daily life within the village and further afield in the western part of The Gambia.

The resources can be used to compile a Big Book of 'Living in Mandinari, The Gambia', with vocabulary lists and the children's questions and comments. Encourage the children to use the resources to develop a presentation on why they would like to visit Mandinari.

Photocopiable pages
The emphasis of the photocopiable pages is pictorial, to make them inclusive and appropriate for most KS1 children. As a result they are able to form the basis of formative assessment of the children's geographical skills and understanding, rather than simply of their literacy skills.

Geography skills
The focus of this chapter is on developing graphicacy skills – the essentially pictorial communication of spatial information – since a pictorial approach is inclusive and appropriate for most children of this age.

NOTES ON THE CD-ROM RESOURCES

Lamin Darboe's family

The family comprises grandmother, Sangi Ceesay, her son Alhagie Ceesay and her adopted son, Lamin Darboe, the orphaned son of her late brother. There's also Lamin's second wife Rohey (Muslims can have up to four wives in The Gambia), Rohey's 14-year-old daughter Kadi, adopted from Rohey's older sister, and Lamin's and Rohey's three-year-old daughter Nicola. This photograph illustrates a small extended family with its strong sense of caring.

In this society, the men are looked upon as providers and produce cash crops or have jobs of 'high' economic value such as small shops or market stalls selling imported goods. Lamin works as a messenger in the capital, Banjul, but also grows watermelons for sale. Alhagie is studying at the new University in The Gambia. The women do the daily 'grind' – cooking, washing, housework, vegetable and fruit growing for family use, and selling any surplus in the local market, as well as looking after the very young children. The other children are looked after by those slightly older than themselves. Everyone has responsibilities and is cared for.

Discussing the photograph
- Discuss why the family are sitting in the shade of some trees.
- Identify the individuals in the photograph.
- Talk about the different generations of the family, using appropriate 'titles' such as *daughter* and *granddaughter*.
- Ask the children to look at the clothes the people are wearing in the photograph. (The women are wearing traditional dress but the men wear western clothes.)
- Encourage the children to talk about their own extended family.

Activities
- Ask the children to draw and name each member of Lamin's extended family.
- Arrange the drawings in age order.
- Rearrange them as a family tree.
- Ask the children to draw and label a picture of their own family (with sensitivity!).

Where is The Gambia?

This image shows the tropical location of The Gambia. From an image of the continent of Africa the country of The Gambia is located. A closer view shows The Gambia surrounded by another country, Senegal. The Gambia is located approximately midway between the Tropic of Cancer and the Equator.

Discussing the picture
- Talk about the picture and what it shows, using the words *world*, *continent* and *country*.
- Explain that the 'globe' shows the continent of Africa and that The Gambia is a country in Africa.
- Identify and use the terms *Equator* and *Tropic of Cancer*. Use the words *north*, *east*, *south* and *west* to describe the location of The Gambia within Africa.
- From its location, encourage the children to suggest what the climate is like.

Activities
- Compare the two-dimensional images of the resource with a three-dimensional globe.
- Locate the continent of Africa and the country of The Gambia on the globe and in a world atlas.
- Compare The Gambia with the UK in terms of size, distance and direction.
- Look up the current weather forecast for The Gambia using, for example, the website www.bbc.co.uk/weather/world/.

Pictorial map of western Gambia

This pictorial map shows the position of Mandinari and the other settlements mentioned here, notably the capital city Banjul and the biggest urban area Serekunda. The urban area of Banjul

A VILLAGE IN THE GAMBIA

is constrained in growth by effectively being an island, but Serekunda can sprawl. From the map you can see that the area is also surrounded by areas of mangrove and mudflats (with many creeks or *bulons*), forest or woodland, cultivation or grassland, and beaches which attract tourists.

When looking at the photographic resources it is useful to refer back to this map and the map of Mandinari to help the children to locate and visualise (an important word for distant locality work) where things are happening.

Discussing the map
▶ Identify the River Gambia and the Atlantic Ocean.
▶ Talk about the north and south banks of the river and which way the river is flowing – it is tidal in this area, but the river flows westward.
▶ Locate Mandinari, Serekunda and Banjul.
▶ Discuss land-use and the meaning of the different colours and symbols, relating them to the key. Encourage the children to describe where each type of land-use is located – for example, the cultivated areas surround the settlements, the mangroves are along the river or bulon banks.
▶ Follow the roads and describe a journey from Mandinari to Serekunda and to Banjul.

Activities
▶ Introduce the idea of making a similar pictorial map of the area of your school – what pictures and colours would you use?
▶ Ask the children to make such a map, possibly working in pairs for support.
▶ Make a land-use map from an aerial photograph of your school. To make the land-use map from the aerial photograph ask the children to place a black and white photocopy of the aerial photograph in a clear plastic sleeve. Trace over the photograph with washable OHP pens and then make a paper photocopy of the tracing. Ask the children to identify the different land-uses in the photo and colour them on the photocopy – for example, playground, houses, school, roads.

Map of Mandinari

This sketch map of Mandinari is based on one drawn by a young man who lives in the village. It shows the locations of compounds – plots of land on which people live; women's gardens (we would call them allotments); schools (primary and Arabic); mosques and many other features. Lamin's compound is just off the map, to the south.

The local language, Mandinka, is essentially a spoken language, therefore there are various spellings of the village name: Mandinari, Mandinary, Mandinaring.

Discussing the map
▶ Ask the children what they can see.
▶ Draw the children's attention to the network of roads (they are more like sandy paths), the various landmarks or buildings, and the water to the north (Mandinari Bulon) and east (River Gambia).
▶ Point out the key and talk about its purpose.
▶ Ask the children to count how many shops there are in Mandinari. How do they know which buildings are shops. Encourage them to use the key.
▶ Ask why there are symbols for 'wells' and 'taps'. What does this tell us about the village?
▶ Notice the areas for women's gardens (allotments). What might be grown there?

Activities
▶ Compare this map with the photocopiable resource on page 57, 'Land-use map of Mandinari' – another map of the village drawn by a boy who lives in Mandinari.
▶ Describe the distributions of the different land-uses and suggest explanations for why they are positioned there. (The 'right answer' is relatively unimportant, it's the thinking behind explanations that is significant.)
▶ Ask the children to produce a map of their school. Encourage them to think about where the roads go and where buildings are positioned. More able children can be asked to draw a map of their local area, with their school in the centre.

Lamin's compound

The house is a long mud-brick single-storey structure, a row of six rooms all used as bedrooms, with a wide verandah and a corrugated tin roof. In the bedrooms there are straw-mattressed beds with mosquito netting, decorated tin trunks for belongings, a water container and oil lamps. Some rooms, which all have corrugated tin doors and window shutters, are subdivided to provide a living-room space at the front. The floor is mud, concrete or lino.

There is very little furniture – a low table and a couple of wooden armchairs with loose cushions which are usually brought on to the verandah. Rohey has a treadle sewing machine and a television in her room. The television runs off a Landrover battery which has to be recharged at Lamin (village). Outside is a screened-off, open-air bathroom area; fruit trees (mostly paw-paw) are irrigated with the used water. Washing water is fetched from the compound's well in a bucket, and ladled from the bucket using a plastic cup or tin can.

Around the building is a dry, sandy garden area with a well, a long-drop toilet, shade trees and the kitchen. Food is prepared on the verandah and cooked on wood fires in the kitchen. The compound area needs to be well-fenced to keep out the goats. The hole that was dug to get the mud for the bricks that built the house is being used as a rubbish pit.

Discussing the photograph

▶ Ask the children what they can see in the picture.
▶ Invite them to suggest what is behind the doors.
▶ Ask the children why they think the people are sitting in the shade outside.
▶ Talk about what the rest of the building is like and what it is made of.
▶ Invite the children to compare it with their own homes.

Activities

▶ Ask the children to draw a picture of the rooms in their own house.
▶ Challenge the children to draw a plan of their own house and make a list in or beside each room of the activities that are done there.
▶ Ask the children to discuss, in pairs, what it would be like living in Lamin's house – the good things and the not so good.

Rohey's kitchen

This is a picture of Rohey working outside her kitchen. She has a plastic bucket on an upturned wooden mortar (of a pestle and mortar), and an aluminium cooking pot to her right. Her adopted daughter, Kadi, is doing the washing in the background. The colourful plastic kettle at the foot of the tree is used to hold water, especially for ablutions before Muslim prayer.

Nearly all Gambians use aluminium cooking pots on fuelwood fires to prepare their food. But The Gambia has no natural resources to produce their own pots and imports are expensive. So by ingenious methods an economic opportunity has resolved the situation. Aluminium scrap is collected (drinks cans from incoming aircraft and hotels, broken cooking pots and aluminium castings from engines) and in very small, dangerous workshops under corrugated tin roofs, the scrap metals are converted into new cooking pots and utensils.

Discussing the photograph

▶ Ask the children what they can see in the picture.
▶ Invite them to suggest what it might be like inside the kitchen (dark and smoky). Note that there is hardly any light inside it and that there are no windows in the wall.
▶ Invite the children to make comparisons with their own kitchen.

Activities

▶ Get the children to draw a plan of their own kitchen. List the activities that take place there.
▶ Find out what the children's families use to cook their food, including the type of cooking utensils and pots and where they are made. What fuel do the children's parents use for cooking? Talk about the similarities and differences between cooking in the UK and The Gambia.
▶ Find out about recipes for Gambian food (see www.africanculture.dk/gambia/foodmenu.htm). Be aware that peanuts/groundnuts and groundnut oil are a major ingredient in much Gambian food, so you may need to adapt the recipes.

A VILLAGE IN THE GAMBIA

The women's gardens

In The Gambia, the women are responsible for growing the fruit and vegetables for family use while the men grow crops that are sold. The women grow their produce in well-fenced (against goats) gardens – we would probably call them allotments. Some gardens are cooperatives, others are worked by women in a group called a 'kafu'. These are friendship and/or age groups. The women often work at their garden all day, even through the midday heat. The woman whose plot is being dug, hoed, planted or harvested provides the food for the whole group for the day, then it is someone else's turn the next day.

The gardens have to be watered by hand with water drawn from a well which is often very deep. It is hard, hot work. The photograph shows young plants being watered, using a tin with holes in it. The well is in the small mound behind the woman's left shoulder.

Discussing the photograph
▶ Talk about what is happening in the photograph.
▶ Notice the neat, small beds with raised walkways that trap the water.
▶ Notice the fence to keep out the goats.
▶ Ask the children if they or their parents grow any vegetables.

Activities
▶ Visit a greengrocer's shop or the vegetable section of a large supermarket and find out which foods come from tropical Africa (mostly Kenya).
▶ Find out what all these fruits and vegetables look like.
▶ For a whole-school project, help the children to establish a school garden or adopt an allotment. Divide it into many small plots and grow fruit trees and vegetables, enlisting parental help to maintain it.

Rice harvesting

Rice is one of The Gambia's staple foods. The Gambians cannot grow enough for their own use, so they have to import it. Families buy 25kg sacks, which cost about £14 each (in 2005). One sack would last Lamin's family about a month. Mandinari has land suitable for growing rice: low-lying land near the tidal River Gambia, but not inundated by salt water. It is watered by rainfall in the rainy season, not by irrigation. The rainy season is usually characterised by one good downpour a day (or night), not by continual rain, but it is unbearably humid.

The photograph shows a women's group, 'kafu', harvesting their rice. This is done by hand, with a knife, one stalk at a time! The green rice plants can be seen in the background. Gambian rice is a cereal crop with a much lower yield than our cereals.

Discussing the photograph
▶ Ask the children what the rice plants look like.
▶ Notice that all the work is being done by hand, there is no machinery (although there are a few tractors for hire for more inland fields).
▶ Notice that the rice is grown on flat land where the vital rain will not run off, but soak into the ground.
▶ Encourage the children to talk about rice, how and when they eat it and which rice meals they particularly like. (In Mandinari most people eat the rice with their right hand, rolling it in a ball with 'soup' – we would call it sauce.)

Activities
▶ Collect different types of rice from supermarkets and health food shops. Which part of the plant do we eat? Find out where the rice comes from, mark the places on a world map or globe and explain the distribution. Are they all from tropical or sub-tropical localities? Is there any rice from The Gambia in our shops?
▶ Collect rice recipes from around the world and try to cook some of them with your class. Alternatively, see if you can persuade the school cook (if you have one) to have a special 'rice day'.
▶ Find out about oats, wheat, barley and rye; how, when and where they are grown and what we use them for. Which part of the plant do we eat?

A VILLAGE IN THE GAMBIA

A mosque in Mandinari

The Gambia is about 90% Muslim (9% Christian and 1% traditional), so there are many mosques of all sizes. Mandinari's main mosque, in the centre of the village, is small. In a room at the back are two village coffins (one adult, one child-size) which are re-used for all deaths and burials). The muezzin can be heard five times a day, calling Muslims to prayer.

Before prayer, Muslims perform ablutions (ceremonial washing of parts of the body). Water is not 'on tap' in Mandinari, so many Gambian men use a colourfully striped plastic 'kettle' (of the traditional shape) as a water container. The lid keeps the water clean and the spout enables the flow to be controlled. At home, Alhagie and Lamin put their prayer mat on the floor of their room or in the open when it is time for prayer. The prayer mat faces to the east, towards Makkah. Sangi and the other women tend to pray in their rooms.

Discussing the photograph
▶ Ask the children to describe the building and suggest what it is and what it is used for. Talk about religious buildings near the school – how and when they are used and by whom. The main prayers of the week are at 2pm on Friday in Mandinari.
▶ Talk about how Muslims observe the requirement to pray five times a day and how ablutions precede prayer.

Activities
▶ Invite a visitor (an Imam [a Muslim priest] or other Muslim) to come and talk to the children.
▶ Read photocopiable page 58, 'Nfansu's morning'.
▶ Act out the story told by Nfansu Touray about early morning in Mandinari (see photocopiable page 58).

Mandinari nursery school

In this photograph, the children are queuing outside the privately run nursery school for measles vaccinations. Most of these children are four years old, but their day is very formal and they usually have to wear a school uniform (green gingham). Even three-year-olds have Arabic phonics lessons. At the nursery school the children use chalkboards and scraps of paper. Every bit of work they do has an encouraging comment written on it and is sent home to the parents. Resources are very scarce. Although there is a library of books donated by tourists, there is no system for using or borrowing the books.

The nursery school can be found in the south of the village of Mandinari, next to the clinic and Arabic school (see photocopiable page 57).

Discussing the photograph
▶ Tell the children where this picture was taken and what is happening.
▶ Ask the children if they know why it is important to have vaccinations.
▶ Encourage the children to talk about health, visits to the doctor and any memories they may have of injections.

Activities
▶ Invite a health visitor or nurse to visit the class to talk to the children about health and hygiene.
▶ For fieldwork, arrange a visit to the nearest health centre or clinic, encouraging the children to find it on a map and plan the route themselves.
▶ Malaria is one of the most serious illnesses for children in The Gambia. Many young children's lives could be saved if they had impregnated bed nets to keep them safe from mosquitoes at night. Arrange a fundraising event to raise money to provide some bed nets for the children at Mandinari nursery or primary school.

Mandinari primary school

This is Grade 5 at Mandinari primary school. Progression is by ability (to pass tests and to pay school fees) not age – so classes can be of very mixed ages. Some children miss school for several years and return when they can afford to. Admission to the next stage of schooling

46   READY RESOURCES ▶▶ GEOGRAPHY

A VILLAGE IN THE GAMBIA

is by examination – there are not enough places available for everyone, but the government is making big efforts to improve access, especially for girls.

Resources are poor, but the children are desperate to learn. There are so many children at this school that classes operate on a shift system. The classrooms are in long, low blocks with air bricks for windows. They are arranged on two sides of a large, hard sandy space which is the football pitch. There are three tin huts at the back for toilets and a water pump which the children operate. There was a school garden where the children were taught to grow vegetables, but it is neglected now because it is too expensive to maintain the fence against goats that roam the village.

Teachers do not apply for their jobs, they are sent to them by the Ministry of Education. This means that a headteacher can be moved to another job at any time, so continuity is a problem. This also impacts on UK schools who want to forge links with a Gambian school.

Discussing the photograph
▶ Ask the children what they notice about the classroom and encourage them to compare it with their own. Remind them of the Gambian children's positive attitude to education and their thirst for knowledge.
▶ Talk about what is in the classroom and discuss how this compares to the resources in the children's own classroom.

Activities
▶ Find the primary school (to the west) on the map of Mandinari village (see above).
▶ For a very short time try to replicate a Mandinari classroom – without using any resources except for paper and pencils, sitting Victorian schoolroom style, standing when a visitor enters the room and with all the children trying their very best with their work!

Nicola and Kadi ready for school

Rohey's daughter Nicola, a three-year-old Muslim girl, is in her uniform for the Arabic school and Kadi is in her uniform for the primary school. Rohey has to work hard to get her children's clothes ready for school. She has no access to running water, convenient washing machines and electric irons (she uses a plastic bowl for washing and a charcoal iron).

Discussing the photograph
▶ Remind the children who the girls are in the picture.
▶ Talk about school uniforms. Ask the children what they think are the good and bad things about uniforms.
▶ Talk about other groups of people who wear uniforms such as nurses, police, soldiers, shop employees and so on. Why do these people wear uniforms?

Activities
▶ Do the children wear a school uniform? If they do, ask them to draw pictures of themselves wearing their uniforms. If they don't, suggest that they draw a picture of the uniform they would like to have.
▶ Where do our clothes come from? Encourage the children to look at the labels in their uniforms or other clothes and find out where they were made.
▶ Make a collection of items of clothing and a list of the items and countries they come from. Locate the countries on a map or globe. Where do most clothes come from?

Water supply

Mandinari does not have a piped water supply. There are boreholes, pumps, wells and standpipes with taps. In some other villages the borehole pumps (often gifts from the Catholic Agency for Overseas Development [CAFOD] or the Arab Emirates) are solar-powered (as a result of aid from the EU). The photograph shows a well in a compound (not Lamin's – he has a simple, uncovered, hole in the ground). There is a simple pulley to help pull the bucket up from the depths. This well is on the point of collapse, as can be seen by the cracked slabs on the right. A new one is being dug.

A few well-buckets are made from recycled lorry inner tube, stitched together, but most are now imported plastic buckets or recycled cooking oil drums. The animals in the photograph are sheep (their tails and ears point downwards). They look very similar to the goats but goats' tails and ears point up! The trees in the background are citrus – the green fruit can just be seen.

Discussing the photograph
- Encourage the children to identify the well, the citrus trees and the sheep.
- Ask the children what the well is for, and why it is there.
- Ask the children to think about what we use water for. Do the children know where we get our water from? How does it get to our tap?
- What would it be like living in a house without a piped water supply? Tell the children how people in most of The Gambia, even young children, have to carry water to their houses.
- Talk about droughts and the effect of these on some parts of Africa.
- Discuss the importance of clean water.

Activities
- Ask the children to try to keep a record of all the ways they, and their family, use water in a weekend.
- Sort the list of uses of water into those that require clean water and those for which recycled water, such as bath water, could be used.
- Discuss ways of saving and recycling water in school. Ask the children to help you to develop a sustainable water-use policy.
- Remind the children that water has to be pumped and carried in The Gambia. Discuss how heavy water is. Challenge the children to work out how heavy a bucketful of water is. Provide measuring jugs and scales and start by measuring out 1000ml and weighing it.

Shopping in Mandinari

The photograph shows the shop in the centre of Mandinari. There are a few smaller shops elsewhere in the village. The shop is at the centre of Mandinari village (see above). Some of the village market stalls are on the road in front of the shop. These are run every morning by the women to sell any surplus fresh produce from their gardens. The shop, run by a Mauritanian trader, sells imported goods such as rice, sugar (both in 25kg sacks), matches and cigarettes, candles, toiletries, coffee, margarine (in small wraps of paper), locally produced soft drinks, and bread (which is similar to French sticks).

Discussing the photograph
- Ask the children what they can see and what they think is happening. You may need to tell them that it is a shop and part of the market.
- Encourage the children to compare it with shops and markets at home and seek explanations for the similarities and differences.
- Explain that the produce on the central table will have been carried to the market in the blue bucket, balanced on the woman's head.
- What do the children think the children sitting in the shade of the verandah are doing?

Activities
- Compare this picture with the pictures of Serekunda market provided on the CD. Talk about the similarities and differences between the markets and shops.
- Set up a classroom market to sell fresh fruit and vegetables, perhaps as part of a 'healthy eating' project, just before break time. Ask the children to identify the fruit and vegetables that could be sold at different times of year.
- Let the children try carrying plastic containers of food on their heads on a ring of cloth.
- Find out where the fruit and vegetables in our supermarkets come from at different times of the year. Mark the information on a world map and find out about seasonal food in the UK.
- Introduce the notion of 'food miles' and the transport and environmental costs of importing food. Would we notice any effects on our lives if we did not import fruit and vegetables?

Mandinari's river and creek

Mandinari village is near the River Gambia. Between the village and the river are mudflats and creeks lined with mangrove. Mangrove plants have specially adapted roots and leaves that

enable them to thrive in tropical saline (salty) wetlands. Around Mandinari, the local people harvest oysters attached to the aerial roots. The shellfish are cooked and eaten, and the shells are burned, crushed and turned into white house-paint. Crabs, molluscs and mudskipper fish living in the mud can be seen at low tide. Monkeys and birds live in the trees.

Ferry and tourist boats called pirogues occasionally come from Banjul to Mandinari 'bridge' or jetty which is to the north of the village. Children also swim there in the salty water. Local fishermen use dug-out canoes to get around.

Discussing the photograph
▶ Talk about the creek (Mandinari Bulong), the vegetation and the effect of the tides.
▶ Ask the children to describe what they can see in the photograph.
▶ Talk about salt and fresh water and discuss the children's experiences or knowledge of rivers, bridges, jetties and tides.

Activities
▶ Visit a waterside location – a river, stream, docks or coast – with a bridge, a jetty or a pier.
▶ Look at a map of The Gambia and identify the River Gambia. Together, find out where its source is.
▶ Make dug-out canoes and other types of boats for floating and loading activities.

Mandinari in the rain

This picture shows baobab trees in Mandinari during a September downpour. The Gambia's sub-tropical climate has distinct dry and rainy seasons. The dry season (November to May) has average temperatures around 21–27°C. The rainy season (June to October) has high humidity and average temperatures around 26–32°C. Temperatures are coolest along the coast. In the rainy season it does not rain continuously – there is usually a daily downpour with sunshine the rest of the day.

Discussing the photograph
▶ Ask the children what is happening in the photograph. Can they explain why it is so green?
▶ What do the children think the landscape might look like in the dry season? How does it change when it rains? When do the children think that most of the food is grown and why?
▶ Ask the children to think about and discuss what they do, wear, play and feel when it rains.

Activities
▶ Let the children take photographs of their local area in dry and in wet weather. Make comparisons, identifying similarities, differences and change.
▶ Compare The Gambia's two seasons with our four. How does the children's local area change from one season to the next? How do people's activities change?
▶ Ask the children to consider how the weather affects their lives. What can or can't they do in different sorts of weather?

Shopping in Serekunda, Serekunda's indoor market

Shopping opportunities in Mandinari are very limited. For anything other than fresh food and very basic everyday needs it is necessary to travel to Lamin village, to Serekunda or possibly to Banjul (although Serekunda has most things from local produce to imported goods).

Lamin buys shoes from Serekunda's indoor market. Rohey travels to Serekunda to meet friends and buy material to have clothes made by the village tailor, but she now has a sewing machine and is learning to make her own clothes. Rohey gets any fresh fruit or vegetables she needs to buy, rather than grow herself, from Mandinari or Lamin markets. However, she might buy fresh meat or fish, or smoked or dried fish in Serekunda (but this is expensive).

Serekunda market has two distinct parts – the indoor market where (mostly) men sell imported goods like clothes and electrical goods, and an outdoor market where (mostly) women sell food. Second-hand clothes sell particularly well.

To get to Lamin village Rohey gets a bush taxi (beat-up Landrovers or minibuses) along the recently tarred road. The fare is 5 dalasi each way. (One dalasi is about 2p.) For Serekunda she would travel to Lamin and then change to a packed minibus for the 5-dalasi journey.

Serekunda is also the transport hub of The Gambia south of the River Gambia. Bush taxis travel to all the local places and mini-buses go from Serekunda to everywhere in the southern part of the country.

Discussing the photographs
▶ Ask the children if they can tell what Lamin is doing.
▶ Where do the children go to buy their shoes?
▶ Talk about the sorts of shops that the children can see in the photograph.
▶ Ask the children what is being sold in the markets. (Note small mosque in background.)
▶ Encourage the children to talk about their own experiences of markets.

Activities
▶ For fieldwork, visit a local indoor, outdoor or farmers' market to see what is for sale. Try to follow or draw a map of the market.
▶ Make a visit to a shopping street near the school. Take a photograph of each shop to look at later. Write down the children's observations and questions about the shops.
▶ Locate Mandinari, Lamin and Serekunda on each of the maps (see above) and try to describe Lamin's or Rohey's journey to Serekunda.
▶ Talk about the different materials that shoes can be made out of.
▶ Develop the work on shoes as a numeracy link by counting in 2s and discussing shoe sizes. Is there a relationship between shoe size and height? Take measurements of the children's heights and foot lengths. Collate it into a chart or diagram.

Getting around

This photograph shows the main crossroads in Serekunda at a fairly quiet time. There are shops on three corners, the market on one (front left) and the mosque (back left). The yellow car with green stripes is a local taxi.

Discussing the photograph
▶ Ask the children what is happening in the photograph. How many different ways are people getting around? How are most people travelling and why?
▶ Talk about the many different ways that people are transporting things around – carrying trays, carrying bowls on their heads, using school bags, a barrow, bicycles, taxis and cars.
▶ Ask the children how they get around.

Activities
▶ Make a list of the different ways of getting around that the children use. For each way, list the place and purpose of the journey. Do the children notice any patterns? For example, which forms of getting around are used for the longest and shortest journeys? Is the most appropriate method used for each journey?
▶ Ask each child to draw a picture of how she or he gets to school. Invite them to colour in their route to school on a map.
▶ Compile a class 'journey to school' map, using a different colour for each form of transport. Identify any patterns.
▶ Find out about the 'walking bus' system and discuss the advantages and disadvantages of introducing one at your school.

Being a Muslim

The photograph (taken December 2003) shows the main junction in Serekunda at 2pm on a Friday – the main Muslim prayers of the week. The mosque, one minaret just visible back left, is too small, so there is overflow into the street. The crowd consists solely of men and boys, praying barefoot, facing Makkah. A huge new mosque, built away from the centre of town so that traffic is not brought to a standstill, was completed in 2004.

Discussing the photograph
▶ Explain to the children what is happening in the picture. Muslim children in your class will, of course, be able to explain the picture to others.

A VILLAGE IN THE GAMBIA

▶ Talk about the impact of this activity on the town (and how it brings the town to a halt). Can the children think of any solutions for preventing this standstill? (Tell them about the completion of the new mosque away from the centre of town.)
▶ Ask the children if they can describe other faiths' forms of worship.

Activities
▶ Mark places of worship on a local map, discussing with the children what would be the appropriate symbol to use for each faith. Ask the children how they will remember what each symbol means, illustrating the need for a key. Make a key together.
▶ Make a visit to a mosque (or a different place of worship).
▶ Use a world atlas (first, because it has an index) and then a globe to locate Makkah.
▶ Together, work out which direction Makkah is in, from the UK.

Banjul

Banjul is the capital city of The Gambia. In colonial times it was called Bathurst. Lamin works in Banjul as a messenger for the Gambian Nurses and Midwives Council. He travels there daily from Mandinari by three bush taxis and minibuses – Mandinari to Lamin, Lamin to Serekunda, Serekunda to Banjul. It is virtually impossible for him to estimate how long the journey will take. The total fare is not much less than he earns for a day's work.

When President Jammeh was elected, he built a huge structure called Arch 22 over the main road into Banjul. From this Arch there is a good view over the city, often marred by dust and heat haze. The photograph is an oblique aerial view of Banjul from the arch, showing settlement, roads, the main mosque and minarets (a fairly new one built away from the town centre). The River Gambia is in the distance, with the port on the south bank (left of the mosque) and the river bank near Mandinari just visible.

Discussing the photograph
▶ Explain to the children that this is Banjul, the capital city of The Gambia. Can the children name the capital city of their own country?
▶ Ask the children what they can see in the photograph.
▶ Do the children think they would like to live there?
▶ Ask the children how Banjul looks similar to and different from a city in the UK.

Activities
▶ Find Banjul on the maps provided. Where do the children think Arch 22 is?
▶ Follow the route Lamin would use to get to Banjul. Ask the children to describe what he would pass.
▶ For fieldwork, try to visit a high building to look down on a town or city near you. Encourage the children to make a 'field sketch'.
▶ Challenge the children to find out about the capital city of their own country – what are the characteristics of a capital?

Banjul street scene

This is the main road that goes into and leaves Banjul (looking in the direction of leaving the city, walking towards Arch 22). It shows a typical wide street with pavement. On the road are taxis and minibuses. On the left, the collection of minibuses is the depot for buses to the small town of Bakau. On the pavement is a woman carrying her baby in traditional style on her back, with a bundle on her head. The man in front of her, in Muslim dress, is carrying live chickens. Behind the wall, on the right, is the Royal Victoria Teaching Hospital.

Discussing the photograph
▶ Ask the children to describe what they can see in the photograph.
▶ Draw their attention to the features mentioned above.
▶ This street is one of the most 'western' in The Gambia. Encourage the children to compare it with their own street or one in a nearby town.
▶ Why is the man carrying live chickens? (Explain that chickens need to be live if they are to be sold for meat as the heat would make them 'go off' quickly in the absence of domestic fridges.)

A VILLAGE IN THE GAMBIA

Activities
▶ Compare this photograph to the street scene of Serekunda (see above). What are the differences and similarities between the two places?
▶ Ask the children to bring in a doll or teddy and tie it to their back for them to carry it Gambian-style for a day. What are the advantages and disadvantages for the mother and the child? Challenge the children to carry something on their heads at the same time!
▶ Ask the children to draw a 'matching' picture of the street, but convert it into a UK view, with British housing, buses, clothing, modes of carrying a baby and shopping. Start the children off with some lines to represent the road and pavement.
▶ Encourage the children to think of, or imagine, a street in their own capital city. Ask them to draw it and compare it with this street in Banjul. Alternatively, provide a photograph or postcard of a city in the UK for them to compare.

The River Gambia

The River Gambia gave the country its name and was one of the major slave routes in the past (Alex Haley's book *Roots* [Vintage] is based in The Gambia). The river used to be the main transport route inland, before a road was built the length of the country.

This view, taken on the river bank behind the market in Banjul, shows the Port of Banjul, the main point of import and minimal export. It also shows the ferry between Banjul on the south bank and Barra on the north – a very much less-developed settlement. On the right are some of the traditional wooden pirogues. These are for hire as ferries to smaller settlements, for the transport of goods, people and animals. Beyond the pirogues is the rusting hulk of a 'dead' ferry. Pelicans can often be seen on this shore, as well as dolphins in mid-river.

Discussing the photograph
▶ Explain to the children that this photograph shows the River Gambia. Tell them where the photograph was taken from.
▶ Ask the children to describe what they see in the picture.
▶ Invite the children to imagine that they are there. What sounds would they hear? What would the weather be like?

Activities
▶ Locate and follow the River Gambia on available maps. Describe its relationship to Banjul, Serekunda and Mandinari.
▶ Find out where the nearest dock or port is to your school. How busy is it? Where do the ships come from and go to? Find out what goods they bring in and take out of the country.
▶ Ask the children to find out where the nearest ferry is (or was) to your school. Why is it there? If it has been replaced (by a bridge) why did this happen?
▶ Discuss the difference in function between a ferry and a ship (and other sorts of boat).

Children playing

In rural areas in The Gambia (and possibly in towns too) children have little access to toys. They make their own, often from materials discarded by tourists. They usually get great satisfaction from them. Sometimes they are given toys by well-meaning tourists. This picture of children playing should interest the children and help them to appreciate how lucky they are.

Discussing the photograph
▶ Ask the children to describe what they see in the picture.
▶ Encourage the children to think about their own toys. Ask them what kind of toys they like to play with.
▶ Ask the children to think about how much they need all of their toys. Suggest that they ask themselves how much they want and how much they need.
▶ Emphasise the importance of sharing toys in play.

Activities
▶ Discuss where and what the children play, indoors and outdoors. Who do they play with? Where are their favourite play places? Why? What are their favourite toys? Why?

A VILLAGE IN THE GAMBIA

- Create a play map of your local area. On a map of the local area identify play spaces and record who plays in each, and what they play.
- Ask the children to give each play space a play rating (like the star system for hotels). What makes a play space special?
- Encourage the children to make some toys from discarded materials.

MUSIC IN THE GAMBIA

Drums

Music – traditional and electronic, plays a very important part in Gambian life. Drums, in particular, are used in village rituals and ceremonies. The photograph shows a small child playing on a drum at a tourist stall in Albert Market, Banjul. Many tourists buy a large drum to take home with them.

Discussing the photograph
- Ask the children what they see in the picture.
- Talk about what the drums are made from.
- Where do the children think the wood comes from? Talk about the possible impact of tourist trade on deforestation.

Activities
- Talk about the things we use wood for. Where does our wood come from?
- Introduce the issue of deforestation, perhaps using flooding in the Philippines (or any topical example) as a case study.
- Talk about tourism in general and consider together why tourists like to visit The Gambia.

Audio: kora music

Mbalax is the pop music of West Africa, but traditional Gambian – or more correctly Mandinka (an ethnic group found across The Gambia, Mali, Guinea and Senegal) – music is played on traditional Mandinkan instruments. These include the kora, the balaphone and drums. The balaphone is like a wooden xylophone. The kora is a 21-stringed instrument made from a calabash gourd covered in cow-hide with a hard-wood neck and fishing-line strings. For more information and images see www.coraconnection.com/pages/WhatisKora.html and the CD *Senegal – the Rough Guide to the Music of Senegal and The Gambia* for the music of Baaba Maal, Mansour Seck, Tata Dinding Jobarteh and Youssou N'Dour.

Discussing the music
- Play the music to the children and ask them to describe what it sounds like.
- Ask them what they think of the music and why.
- Explain that the main instrument that they can hear is called a kora. Explain what a kora is.

Activities
- Find out about the kora with the children. Ask them to imagine what it looks like. Find a picture of the kora and ask the children to draw it.
- Using the audio clip as a starting point, ask the children to create their own drum music and rhythms.
- Ask the children to improvise a short dance movement to accompany the audio clip or their own drum music.

NOTES ON THE PHOTOCOPIABLE PAGES

Gambia word cards
PAGES 55–56

These cards contain some of the vocabulary for the children to learn and use when looking at life in The Gambia. They include:
- words to develop the children's geographical vocabulary

A VILLAGE IN THE GAMBIA

▶ words associated with The Gambia.
Read through the word cards with the children to familiarise them with the key words of the unit. Ask which words the children have heard before and clarify any they don't understand.

Activities
▶ Cut out and laminate the cards. Use them as much as possible when discussing the pictures and maps.
▶ Shuffle the cards and spread a set of cards on each group's table. Ask the children to find specific words you call out.
▶ Use the cards as a word bank to help the children to label pictures and to help them with longer pieces of writing. Encourage the children to add words to the bank.
▶ Use the word cards and the children's word bank to write captions for all the photographs.
▶ Begin a glossary with the words and include any other topic vocabulary used in the unit.

Land-use map of Mandinari   PAGE 57

This is a land-use map of Mandinari, based on a map drawn by Mbemba Touray who lives in the village. It looks different from the 'Map of Mandinari' because it focuses on different aspects of the village, concentrating on how the land is used, rather than features such as road names and property.

Discussing the map
▶ Tell the children what the map shows.
▶ Talk about the different features that are shown on the map.
▶ Ask the children what kind of pattern they see in the way land is used in Mandinari.

Activities
▶ Encourage the children to study the map and colour it in appropriately.
▶ Ask the children to create their own key for the map.
▶ Compare this photocopiable map with the 'Map of Mandinari' and ask the children how the two maps are similar and different.
▶ Create a land-use map of the children's own school.

Nfansu's morning 6–8am, Nfansu's day   PAGES 58–60

However good we are at 'reading' photographs, it can be difficult to understand the story they tell in situations that are unfamiliar to us. Stories told by people who live in culturally different places can help us. Nfansu lives in Mandinari – in his family's compound on the main street, almost opposite the Muslim cemetery or graveyard. In these stories he describes early morning in his compound and village, and a day in the life of himself and other members of his extended family. Note that the Toubab language is the English language because Toubab means 'white person'.

Discussing the story
▶ Use the photographs from the resource stories to help the children to contextualise the story.
▶ Read the story, explain unfamiliar events and encourage the children to visualise what is happening, and where.
▶ Identify and sequence the events or incidents in the stories.
▶ Compare the stories with the children's own lives.

Activities
▶ Spend some time matching photographs from the CD-ROM resources with aspects of Nfansu's day.
▶ Encourage the children to tell, in words or pictures, the story of their own early morning and a day in the life of their own family.
▶ Dramatise Nfansu's and the children's stories.

Gambia word cards

A VILLAGE IN THE GAMBIA

The Gambia

Africa

Mandinari

Banjul

Serekunda

Gambia word cards

A VILLAGE IN THE GAMBIA

compound

village

mosque

well

field

River Gambia

Land-use map of Mandinari

A VILLAGE IN THE GAMBIA

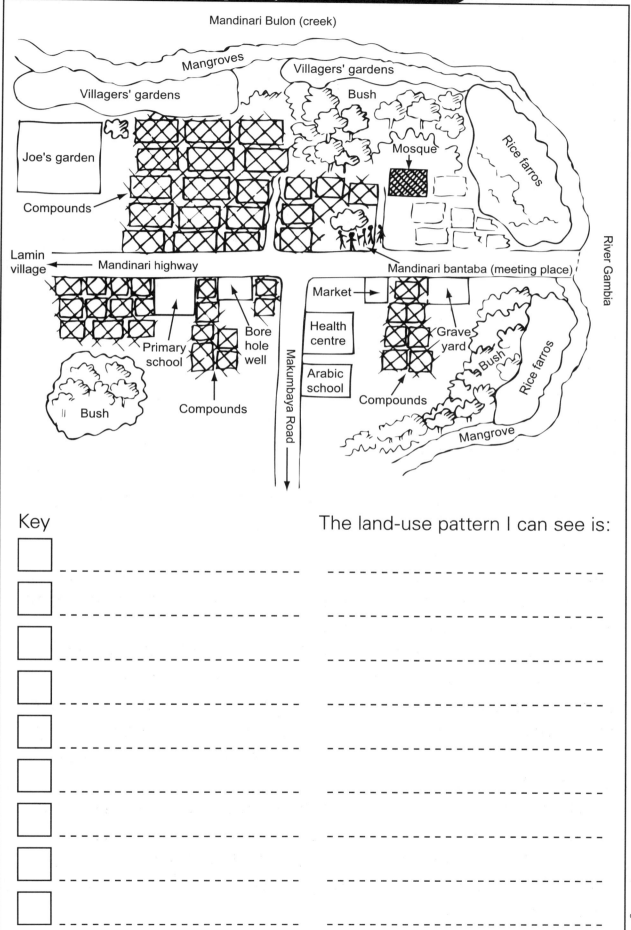

Key

The land-use pattern I can see is:

Nfansu's morning 6-8am

A VILLAGE IN THE GAMBIA

As the first rays of sunlight fall on Mandinari my father wakes to the sound of the early morning cock crow. All is quiet except for the distant call to prayer and the noise of mortar and pestle in some neighbouring compounds. Life slowly returns to the village.

Father wakes mother to prepare breakfast. He proceeds to wash and prepare for early morning prayer at the mosque. The first smoke in the compound rises above the kitchen hut as mother makes the fire. Thumping the pestle into her old and cracked mortar, she adds to the chorus of pounding. This rising and falling tune is carried a considerable distance over the dew-covered bush.

Father walks to the mosque and the prayers can be heard over the loudspeakers that directly face my compound, the blaring sound is a nuisance to late risers like myself. I roll over to lie on my back and stretch, waking up to another long day. After ten minutes father returns and knocks on my bedroom door, commanding me to rise and pray. He then wakes the rest of the family, except for the small children who do not yet pray. It is ten to seven. I turn on the radio to listen to the morning preaching and the news that follows.

Father sits on a small bench upon the veranda saying his prayers, turning his beads constantly through his fingers, staying in this position until mother calls him to breakfast. Sometimes he walks around the backyard praying.

By now mother has made breakfast. Yesterday it was coffee and bread, today it is millet porridge. She lays the bowl in a wide pan of water to cool it quickly, walks outside to sweep the compound's yard and is joined in her work by my sisters. Rising, I do my own prayers, hearing the brooms scratching as I move from position to position.

Minutes later we take our breakfast, men and boys gathered in my father's house, women and girls in the main women's quarters. When they have eaten, the children start to run around everywhere, turning their old bicycle and car tyres frantically, welcoming the new day.

Nfansu's day

A VILLAGE IN THE GAMBIA

After breakfast, mother and my sisters tend their vegetables in the village's co-operative garden. Mother sells surplus tomatoes, aubergines and okra in the village market. Like all the women, she works hard, spending hours each day in the gardens and, in the rainy season, in the rice fields.

Mother gives domestic chores to another of my sisters – fetching water from the hand pump, filling the many jars and buckets in each house within our compound. I hear my sister warning the young children of the punishments they will get if they spill this precious water; she is a strict, hard-working girl.

Today father firmly reminds me to mend the compound fence and to fetch firewood. Two brothers and I take three hours to fix the fence, then rest in the shade of a mango tree, chatting while our sister bustles between the main house and the kitchen, cooking lunch for us all. Children, tired of running about kicking rag balls, are making grass toys or playing simple games upon the house veranda. The hot weather has slowed us all down.

The dry harmattan (the northeasterly trade wind), frequently laden with Saharan dust, parches throats and cracks the lips and skin of those not using body cream. Mornings and evenings are so cool that many refuse to take a bath outdoors.

With my last 5 dalasi (about 10p), I go to buy ataya, a local tea. My brothers walk to the shop with me, joking as we go and inviting friends to join us. Returning home we brew the tea, happy as we discuss everything in the universe.

As we chat my mother and sisters return from their hot work. After a short rest mother leaves for the rice fields (*farros*) to work in her *kafo*. Each village has several *kafo*, groups of women who band together to work in rotation from one member's field to another. They set out together and will eat in the fields – the owner of the day's field cooks for the group.

As we settle down to lunch, father orders two children to rush off and drive birds away from the field near the cows. They go immediately. Two other children return from primary school,

Nfansu's day (continued)

A VILLAGE IN THE GAMBIA

neat in the uniforms they wear to learn their lessons and Toubab language. The boy is in a shirt and black shorts, the girl wears a blue dress with a white belt.

On this *kafo* work-day, my sisters have the afternoon off from work in the rice fields. They sit on chairs placed under the shady orange tree by the compound gate, chatting and laughing. They plait each other's hair and break into song, trying out new popular song 'styles'. I treasure these moments.

The sun dips, the air cools a little. Four o'clock – time to fetch firewood. A friend and I walk a kilometre from the village, spend 30 minutes gathering cooking fuel wood, then search for wild fruit before returning home. Mother is not yet back from her work and father rakes up leaves in the compound. Some sisters pound rice, their deep rhythm rolling under the trees as they lift and drop their long pestles into the mortar bowls carved from tree trunks. My nephews and nieces are being busily bathed in bowls at one end of the compound. Ours is a busy compound as everyone has come to live with our grandparents.

It is quickly getting dark. Mother wearily enters the compound as the faint sound of the Mullah's fourth call to prayer spills over the village from the mosque. In an hour the Mullah will call us for the last of the day's five prayers. Having bathed I relax in my room and read two chapters of a novel as music bellows from my brother's tape recorder.

My sister has prepared domoda for dinner. In the bright moonlight children play games and young girls sing by the compound gate. Mother, very tired, has gone to bed. My sisters sit on mats in the centre of the compound drinking ataya. I wander off to chat and drink ataya at a friend's house. By eleven o'clock the children are asleep and the village is quiet. The silence interrupted only by occasional laughter of neighbours chatting and a few dogs barking.

Just after midnight I walk home by moonlight, prepare my bed, say *Al-hamdu lilah* to yesterday and *Bismillah* to the new day, and fall asleep to the choral song of the millions of insects.

TRAIN RIDE THROUGH EUROPE

Content and skills

This chapter links to the 'continuous' units 5 and 24 of the QCA Scheme of Work for Geography at Key Stage 1 – 'Where in the world is Barnaby Bear?' and 'Passport to the world', respectively. The concept of a train journey provides a structure for the children to learn about places in Europe. The children will learn about the location of these places and how they are connected to each other – but the aim is to balance, rather than reinforce, tourist images of Europe. The journey begins in Amsterdam, with a look at Dutch landscapes and features, and then moves up the Rhine valley, visiting Strasbourg en route. The next stop is in Switzerland, with an excursion on a mountain railway. The final destination is Venice in Italy.

The resources look at the different landscapes that will be encountered on the journey and the common themes of transport and of water (in the form of canals, rivers and waterfalls). Through questioning, the children will develop ideas about the different ways in which people live and work in these places. More able children can build upon the resources by finding out about other countries in Europe.

The teachers' notes contain background information about the resources and include ways of using them as a whole class, for group work, or as individuals. Wherever possible, the activities encourage the children to ask questions and develop an enquiring approach to their learning. Using the resources, discussion points and activities in this chapter will also help to develop children's visual literacy skills and, specifically, their ability to gather information from images and maps.

The activities provide opportunities for geographical enquiry, using teachers' questions following the key question sequence implicit in the National Curriculum. The sequence of questions relates to the level descriptions for assessment purposes:
▶ Where is the locality/place?
▶ What is it like?
▶ Why is it like this?
▶ How does it relate to/compare with other places?
▶ What is the environmental quality of the place like?
▶ How is it linked to other places in the world?

Resources on the CD-ROM

The resources on the CD-ROM provide a wide range of pictorial images from a variety of perspectives, including ground level, oblique and vertical aerial viewpoints. There are pictorial maps as well as photographs and a video clip of Venice.

Photocopiable pages

The photocopiable pages in the book are also provided in PDF format on the CD-ROM and can be printed from there. They include:
▶ word cards containing essential vocabulary for the unit
▶ a worksheet to introduce foreign languages
▶ stories.

Geography skills

This chapter focuses on graphicacy (especially the pictorial communication of spatial information) and developing graphicacy skills through drawing simple sketches to record a landscape. Children will also develop key geographical vocabulary. In addition there are opportunities to develop specific geographical skills, including using maps and secondary sources to ask and answer geographical questions.

NOTES ON THE CD-ROM RESOURCES

Map of Europe

This map of Europe shows the major countries of Europe and their capitals, as well as the route followed in this chapter. The journey begins in Amsterdam, and then moves down the Rhine valley, visiting Strasbourg en route. The next stop is in Switzerland, with an excursion on a mountain railway. The final destination is Venice in Italy.

Discussing the map
▶ Tell the children that this is a map of Europe. Introduce the words *holiday maker* and *tourist*, and the concept of travel.
▶ Point out the major countries in Europe. Indicate the capital cities (marked by square symbols). Do the children know which country they live in?
▶ Trace the rail journey together, showing the children where Amsterdam is. Point out the different stops that will be 'visited' in this resource gallery.

Activities
▶ Enlarge and print out the map. Mark out the stages of the journey as the children go through the resources in this chapter.
▶ For each country that is visited on the journey, invite the children to contribute anything they know about the country and make a list of useful information. Also, make a list of questions the children would like to ask about each country.
▶ Ask the children if they have been on holiday in Europe and mark the places on the enlarged map.

THE NETHERLANDS

Dutch canal and bicycle, Dutch houseboat

The Netherlands, Belgium and Luxembourg are also known as 'The Low Countries' because they are very flat and low-lying. Much of the land has been reclaimed from the sea and some is below the present sea level. The land has to be protected by barriers or mounds of earth called 'dykes' which keep the sea out, although occasionally there are serious floods.

Sometimes the Netherlands is referred to as Holland. However, Holland is not a country but refers to two provinces (North and South Holland) in the Netherlands.

Amsterdam is the capital city of the Netherlands, but the seat of government is in The Hague (the capital of South Holland). The national language is Dutch, although French and German are also spoken. You can travel from the UK to Amsterdam by aeroplane, by ferry (from Newcastle), by rail or by car (via the Channel Tunnel, and through France and Belgium).

These photographs show typical scenes in the old parts of Amsterdam. The city has a network of canals bordered by narrow streets and bridges making car travel difficult. People can use cars here but they often prefer to use bicycles and leave these chained to the railings while they go shopping or go to work. Most streets have special cycle lanes to make travel safer and the air is cleaner than it would be if everyone used cars.

Many tourists use boats on the canals to travel around the old city. There are also working boats that carry goods, such as building materials, from place to place. Some people live on houseboats moored at the sides of the canals – some boats even have gardens on board!

Discussing the photographs
▶ Explain to the children that this is what they would see if they visited Amsterdam. Invite the children to talk about the view and identify some features.
▶ Help the children to understand the idea of *background*, *middle* and *foreground* (or use 'the far part', the 'middle part' and the 'near part' for younger children).
▶ Ask the children what they can see in the background of the canal picture.
▶ Tell the children that some of these buildings are homes and some are hotels. Ask them to describe the houses including the colours, materials used and the shapes of the buildings.

▶ Focus the children on the middle and foreground of both photographs. What kinds of transport are shown in the pictures? What are the different boats used for?
▶ How many cars, boats and bikes can they see in the two pictures?
▶ Talk about the advantages and disadvantages of each of these forms of transport in a big city like Amsterdam.

Activities
▶ Ask the children to draw the form of transport that they would most like to use to travel around Amsterdam. Talk about their reasons for choosing it.
▶ Use coloured sugar-paper to make a display of a canal-side scene. Cut out and add the children's transport to the display.
▶ Make a pictorial bar chart called 'Transport in Amsterdam' based on counting the different types of transport seen in the pictures. Use cut-out shapes of boats, cars and bikes and plot these on a simple chart.
▶ Ask the children to think of words that are linked to the forms of transport in the photographs. Make a sorting game with the words on cards and ask the children to sort them under the headings 'Boats', 'Cars' and 'Bicycles'. For example, Boats – water, canal, float; Cars – petrol, horn, road; Bicycles – pedals, bell, rider.

Dutch houses

This photograph shows a typical residential Dutch street, with a canal running through it. Canals are artificial waterways rather than natural rivers. Amsterdam is famous for its canals and they have a number of important functions: to drain the land, which is essential in low-lying countries; they provide a means of transport from the inland areas to the sea; they are used for holidays and recreation (in cold winters it is possible to ice-skate on them); they act as sewers for many houseboats, which are regularly flushed out. In urban areas, in particular, canals are dirty and the water might be toxic.

Discussing the photograph
▶ Tell the children what the picture shows. Have they ever seen or been to a city or town with a canal?
▶ Ask the children to describe the houses and buildings.
▶ Ask the children to consider in what ways these homes are similar and different to their own homes.

Activities
▶ Compare this photograph to the Dutch canal and bicycle images. In what ways are the locations similar and different?
▶ Use coloured sugar-paper to make Dutch houses. Prepare stencils for the roofs, doors and windows for the children to draw around and cut out. Mount the houses side by side to make a continuous row and display along the canal-side display (as described above).
▶ Ask the children to think of ways in which people can keep the canals cleaner. List their ideas on a board.

Windmill and wind turbine, Dutch countryside

Windmills are a common feature of the Dutch countryside. One of their many uses was to pump water out of the earth, keeping the fields dry enough for crops to grow. Flowers and bulbs are a major export and tourist attraction in spring. Pasture land is widespread and the Netherlands produces dairy products, especially cheeses, as well as bacon, pork and poultry.

Many rural areas still have their old windmills even though modern electric pumps are used nowadays. Farms often have wind turbines to generate the electricity needed for modern farm equipment and the farmhouse. The pictures show the landscape in an area of flat farmland known as a polder. The largest polders exist where a huge area of sea called the Zuider Zee ('zee' meaning sea) was pumped dry to create new farmland and villages.

Discussing the photographs
▶ Tell the children that our 'train' is leaving Amsterdam to travel further into Europe. Show them where we are going on the 'Map of Europe' (across the Netherlands towards Strasbourg).

▶ Ask the children to guess what the countryside of the Netherlands will be like. Write down their ideas. Look at the pictures to see if their ideas were correct.
▶ Compare the different windmills in the photographs. Ask the children how the windmills are similar and different.

Activities
▶ Ask the children to suggest ways in which the Dutch countryside is different from Amsterdam. Make a list of the different features.
▶ Read the story of 'A brave little Dutch boy' (on photocopiable page 77).
▶ Print out the photographs and label the physical and human features with the children's help. Add question captions to attract interest and discussion, such as 'What kind of windmill is this?' or 'What is the weather like?'.

THE RHINE VALLEY AND STRASBOURG

Map of the upper River Rhine

In the next part of the train journey through Europe we travel across The Netherlands to the Rhine valley, which we will follow southwards (upstream) as far as Switzerland. The Rhine flows from its source in the Alps to its mouth in the North Sea at Rotterdam in the Netherlands. The port at the mouth of the Rhine is called Europoort. It is often referred to as the 'gateway to Europe' because from here it is possible to reach many parts of Europe by water transport via the Rhine and the many canals that link it to other major rivers.

This map shows the upper part of the Rhine and its source in Switzerland. The following resources look at scenes along and near the Rhine from the Black Forest to the Rhine Falls at Shaffhausen.

Discussing the map
▶ Explain to the children what this map shows.
▶ Point out the route of the River Rhine.
Ask the children where the source of the River Rhine may be (in the mountains). Can they think why the river would start in the mountains?

Activities
▶ Explain that the 'Map of the Rhine' is a close-up of one part of the 'Map of Europe'. Ask the children to locate the Rhine in Europe.
▶ Demonstrate simply to the children that water flows downhill and that the water in a river moves from the highland, where it begins, to the sea.
▶ Use a sloping length of guttering to show the children that flowing water can move floating objects. Introduce the words *downstream* and *upstream*. Ask the children whether they think it is easier for a barge to move upstream or downstream and why.

The Rhine Valley, Barge on the River Rhine

The most well-known views of the Rhine, which show its huge importance as a routeway, are in a narrow section known as the Rhine 'rift valley', between the Black Forest and the Vosges Mountains. Here the Rhine is always busy with shipping and barges piled high with containers are a common sight. In addition, both banks of the river are lined by main roads and railways.

Motorways, which follow parallel routes, link the large cities such as Bonn, Cologne, Koblenz and Strasbourg, which have developed on the banks of the Rhine. The importance of controlling the river in the past is demonstrated by the number of castles that line the riverbank.

Discussing the photographs
▶ Ask the children to think about a river near where they live. What is it called? What is it like? Are there any boats on it? What do the boats carry?
▶ Look at the photograph of 'The Rhine Valley' together. How is the river similar or different to the river the children know locally?

▶ Ask the children to name all the different ways of travelling that can be seen on the photograph. What are the boats used for?
▶ Look at the long barge. Point out that it is longer than the car park. It is low in the water because it is full. It may be carrying grain or oil.
▶ Now look at the barge in 'Barge on the Rhine' – it is full of containers. How many are there on the barge? (It is as much as around 80 lorry loads.)
▶ Explain to the children that it is cheaper to send goods by one barge than to hire 80 lorries. Can they think of any other reasons to send heavy goods by water (such as less traffic on the roads, cleaner air, fewer people to pay wages to, quieter, a smoother journey for the goods)?

Activities
▶ Make a simple floating barge from balsa wood and float this on the water tray. Ask the children to make containers from LEGO. Invite them to predict how many containers the barge can hold. Test the children's predictions.
▶ Encourage the children to experiment to see how they could change the barge to carry more containers (area, thickness, different materials and so on).
▶ Taste (with consideration of allergies/dietary restrictions) some products grown on German farms in and near the Rhineland – including grapes, black cherries, Black forest ham, cheese and sauerkraut. Look for any German labels and discuss the different words.

Strasbourg

Strasbourg is the next destination. It is in Alsace in the north-eastern part of France. In this part of Europe the border between France and Germany has changed in the past. Strasbourg is the headquarters of the Parliament of the European Union (EU) and it boasts impressive new parliament buildings adorned with the flags of all the countries in the EU.

The EU and the concept of European integration was first proposed by the French Foreign Minister Robert Schuman in a speech on 9 May 1950 to prevent a repeat of the atrocities in the Second World War. The date 9 May is celebrated every year as Europe Day. The first countries to join were: Belgium, Germany, France, Italy, Luxembourg and the Netherlands. The United Kingdom joined in 1973.

The EU flag consists of 12 gold stars in a circle on a blue background. The circle of gold stars symbolises solidarity and harmony, and the number 12 is the traditional symbol of perfection, unity and completeness.

Discussing the photograph
▶ Show the children the picture of all the flags flying outside the parliament building in Strasbourg. Which flags can they identify? Use the Europe map on the CD-ROM to support flag recognition.
▶ Count the flags on the picture and tell the children that they represent countries in the EU. Explain to the children that the countries in the EU have joined together to help each other. Explain that a 'union' is when people or countries join together.
▶ Point out the EU flag and explain what it symbolises.
▶ Note that many of the EU countries use euros, but that the UK still uses pounds.

Activities
▶ Look at the official website of the European Union to find out about the other countries in the European Union and their flags (www.europa.eu.int/index_en.htm).
▶ Use photocopiable page 76, 'Learning about Europe' to show the flags visited in this chapter. Enlarge and colour two flags for each country and attach them back-to-back on one end of a stick.
▶ Use photocopiable page 76 to teach the children to say 'hello' and 'goodbye' in the languages of the five countries featured in this chapter.
▶ Ask each child to find a picture of a European country (using tourist brochures, postcards, magazines and the resources in this gallery). Invite them to write a short caption.

The Rhine Falls

Schaffhausen, near Basle, is in Switzerland and is famous with tourists for its spectacular waterfall (the Rhine Falls). It is possible to take a choppy boat ride into the spray at the base of the falls. Schaffhausen is also where upriver navigation on the Rhine stops. At the nearby city of Basle, barges are unloaded or may already have left the Rhine via adjoining rivers and canals.

Discussing the photograph
▶ Show the children where the Rhine Falls are on the maps. Explain that your journey has now taken you to another country – Switzerland.
▶ Introduce the word *waterfall*, explaining that water flows downhill and that sometimes there is a 'step' made of hard rock which crosses the path of a flowing river. The water falls over this step making a waterfall.
▶ Ask the children to look for the people in the photograph to help establish the scale of the falls.
▶ Explain that boats cannot sail up a waterfall. What would happen if a boat tried to do so? Stress the power and speed of the water.
▶ Ask the children to imagine they are passengers on the boat at the foot of the central rock. What can they see and hear? How do they feel on the boat? Do they feel safe? Ask them to explain their reasons.

Activities
▶ Write a class poem about the Rhine Falls with the children or let them write their own descriptive poems. A model such as an acrostic or haiku poem would work well.
▶ Dramatise the boat journey giving yourself the role of ticket seller and tour guide and the children the role of tourists. Guide them through a safety procedure for the journey, tell them what they will see and encourage them to ask questions about the river and the waterfall.
▶ Help the children to make tourist brochures or posters about visiting the Rhine Falls.

TRAVELLING IN THE SWISS MOUNTAINS

Map of the Bernese Oberland

This map is a representation of the Bernese Oberland, a 70-mile long range of the Central Alps in south-west Switzerland. The pictorial map shows the six major mountain peaks of the area, together with the train routes that join the main settlements. In mountainous areas settlements exist mainly in the valleys and are linked by valley routes. Swiss railway technology and the popularity of the mountain areas with tourists have, however, combined to ensure that some very high mountain locations are served by public transport.

Discussing the map
▶ Ask the children to identify features on the map such as snow, mountains, peaks and valleys. Explain, using the map, that a valley is the lower land between two high places.
▶ Show the children the railway routes on the map and tell them that the dots represent stations and that these stations are Swiss towns and villages.
▶ Talk about tourists and why they might like to go to these mountains.

Activities
▶ Make some prints of the map and challenge small groups to plan a circular train journey. Make a list of the places the train visits, and using Google (images button) on the internet, try to find one picture of each place.
▶ Using light blue sugar-paper as a base, and a suitable palette of colours, let the children choose one of the big mountains to paint a picture of. Frame the pictures with red sugar-paper frames to represent train windows and display them with labels such as 'Jenny saw the Jungfrau from the train'.
▶ Challenge the children to make a simple railway route layout using a Brio wooden train set (or similar). Invite them to show what they have designed on a picture map.

Walking in the mountains, Hang-gliding

Mountains and lakes are the dominant features of the Bernese Oberland. High mountain environments pose enormous difficulties for settlement and travel. In Switzerland, however, technological advances mean that tourists can enjoy an exciting range of travel opportunities. Many people go mountain-walking, climbing and even hang-gliding. The resources in this section illustrate the different travel options and the photocopiable resource 'Heidi in the mountains' offers an historical perspective of life in the Swiss Alps.

Discussing the photographs
▶ Show the children the photograph of the family walking in the mountains and ask them to discuss what the family can see, hear, smell and feel.
▶ Talk about how to keep safe when mountain walking – by keeping to paths, not running downhill, wearing sensible footwear and taking equipment such as a compass, first-aid kit, whistle, map and mobile phone.
▶ Talk about keeping the beautiful environment clean and preserving the wildlife and wildflowers.
▶ Ask the children what they think is happening in the hang-gliding photograph. Tell them that this is an exciting sport and a way of getting down the mountain, but focus them on safety issues!

Activities
▶ Look at a pair of climbing boots and walking poles. Discuss how they work, who uses them, and when they are used.
▶ Ask the children to make a list all the things they would need to go walking in the mountains. Put some examples in a backpack to show them.
▶ Ask the children to make a list of all the healthy foods they might take on a picnic. Read about Heidi's picnic lunch, as described in Chapter 3 of the book *Heidi* by Johanna Spyri (Penguin Popular Classics). Ask the children to compare their ideas with the lunch that Heidi had.
▶ Collect additional images from tourist materials which show leisure activities such as skiing, hang-gliding, paragliding and mountain biking. Produce a display to look at ways of using the mountains as a leisure resource.

Cogwheel railway, Cable car

These photographs show two mechanical ways of ascending mountains. Each type of mechanical transport has its own technology. Cogwheel (or funicular) railways use ground-level vehicles that run on tracks with cogwheels to stop them sliding back (they are also fixed to a cable at ground level and the descending car helps the ascending one to rise). Sometimes bridges are built to even out the slope. Cable cars can also take a lot of people at once – some take more than 100 passengers. They are used to go up vertical cliffs and across valleys. There are two cars fixed to the cable and the weight of the one going down helps the other one to rise.

Discussing the photographs
▶ Show the children each photograph in turn and ask them to name and describe the vehicles shown. Introduce and explain the words *ascending* and *descending*. Do the children think the vehicles are ascending or descending? Why?
▶ Ask the children how they think each one works – what kind of power is used. Do they think it will be noisy or quiet?
▶ Explain simply how each mode of transport works. Use construction equipment to show how cogs grip the tracks.

Activities
▶ Using a range of tourist brochures of the Swiss Alps, ask the children to find pictures of all kinds of transport – from hang-glider to boat. Write headings such as: 'Travels on the ground'; 'Travels in the air'; 'Travels on a cable'; 'Transports one person', and so on. Place your choice of headings in sorting rings and encourage the children to place their pictures in these sets, explaining their reasons.
▶ Ask the children to think about different weather conditions such as deep snow, high winds, thunderstorms and so on. How would the different types of transport be affected by these weather extremes? For example, the trains would need snowploughs; the cable cars and gondolas would sway in the wind and so on.

Swiss village

This photograph shows the village of Lauterbrunnen in the Bernese Oberland, Swizerland. The village is shown on the 'Map of the Bernese Oberland'. The photograph shows the view from the Jungfraubahn train as it begins its climb.

This is one of the most famous valleys in Europe because it shows all the typical features of a valley made by a glacier. The sides of the valley are like vertical cliffs, the valley is narrow and U-shaped, waterfalls plunge over the sides, and the villages are in the bottom of the valley. The surrounding mountains are permanently snowcapped because it is so cold at high altitude. In summer, as the snow melts, it is common to hear avalanches – like loud peals of thunder – in the warmest part of the day.

Discussing the photograph
▶ Explain to the children that this is the type of place they would see if they were travelling through the mountains of Switzerland.
▶ Ask the children what they think it would be like to live in the village in the photograph.
▶ Ask the children how this settlement location differs from their own locality. Where would they prefer to live and why?

Activities
▶ Use pictures cut out from Swiss tourist brochures to illustrate feature words such as *village*, *chalet*, *meadow*, *church*, *valley*, *stream*, *waterfall* and *station*, make a Pelmanism game with pictures on some cards and matching words on others.
▶ Ask the children to imagine they are on holiday in a chalet in Lauterbrunnen. Ask them to write a few sentences about what they can see when they open their bedroom curtains and look outside each morning.
▶ Give each child a photograph of a Swiss chalet (cut out from tourist brochures) and ask them to draw a similar-sized picture of their own home. Stick both pictures side by side on the top of a sheet of paper, then find six things that are similar and six that are different. Vary the number to suit different abilities.

Jungfraubahn

The Jungfraubahn railway carries tourists to the 'Top of Europe' (the highest point on any European railway). It is an electric railway with a rack and pinion traction system, which helps the train to grip the steep slopes. The track winds back and forth on the mountainside to minimise the gradient.

The train leaves Lauterbrunnen and climbs steeply towards the Eiger and Jungfrau mountains. It calls at Wengen, Kleine Shiedegg and Eigergletcher (meaning 'Eiger glacier'), where this photograph is taken. Eventually the train enters the mountainside and travels through a tunnel across the north face of the Eiger to the col between the Eiger and Jungfrau. Here, from the Jungfraujoch, tourists can walk on the glacier, visit an ice palace carved in solid ice, and meet the local mountain dogs. The height at this point is 3454m and the air is so thin that many tourists need time to acclimatise and cannot exert themselves much.

Discussing the photograph
▶ Encourage the children to name any features that they can see in the picture.
▶ How do the children think the train can go up the steep mountain without slipping back? Explain in simple terms how the train operates on a rack and pinion system. Use a wooden cogwheel and track (from technology equipment) to show how this system works and how this enables the train to move up the steep slopes.
▶ Ask the children to imagine that they are on the train. What would it be like? What would they be able to see, hear and smell?

Activities
▶ Use this photograph in conjunction with the photograph of the Swiss village to consider how steep the mountains are.
▶ Use this photograph to develop vocabulary such as *gradient*, *steep*, *tunnel* and so on. Compile word banks relating to the topic.
▶ Compare this railway to other ways of travelling in the mountains.

Eiger Glacier

This photograph shows the Eiger Glacier, which can be seen from the Jungfrau railway and is situated between the Eiger and Mönch. This photograph was taken during the summer, so meandering streams of meltwater can be seen on the ice surface – which is dirty in places where the meltwater has left debris eroded by the glacier. A ridge of debris (a moraine) can be seen in the foreground and its scale can be appreciated from the size of the two hikers.

Discussing the photograph
▶ Tell the children what this picture shows and where the glacier is. Explain what a glacier is, if necessary.
▶ Point out the people in the photograph (two walkers on the footpath) and emphasise how big the mountain is.

Activities
▶ Use the photographs to develop the children's vocabulary. Use such words as: *wildflowers*, *steep*, *peak*, *glacier*, *meltwater*, *rock waste* or *debris*, *footpath* and *avalanche*.
▶ Compare the mountain environment of the glacier with the photograph of the Swiss village. What is the land like near the Eiger Glacier? What can the children see that is not in the valley? What can they see that is also in the valley? Compile a class chart to record the points of comparison.

ITALY

Aerial view of Venice

Helping children to appreciate how things look from the air and on the ground gives them a better understanding of maps. This section starts with an aerial view of Venice. If you can find an aerial perspective of a UK city (especially a familiar one) then this would make a good starting point and comparison.

Venice is one of the world's most beautiful cities. Built on a group of small islands in the north-east of Italy, it is a city where canals take the place of roads and in which nearly all transport is on water. The absence of road traffic and its noise makes Venice a calm and relaxing place to visit. It is a colourful city with magnificent domed churches, ornate palaces and terracotta and ochre-painted shuttered canal-side houses and palaces. These can best be seen along Venice's main 'high street' – the Grand Canal.

Italy is the warmest of the countries visited on our journey across Europe. Summer days are hot and usually dry. The narrow side canals and streets in Venice have been designed carefully to keep the inhabitants shaded and as cool as possible. It hardly ever snows in Venice – but a major hazard for the city is flooding. This occurs regularly after periods of heavy rain and especially at times when snow is melting on the high mountains of the Alpine region. The fear of the sea level rising permanently in this low-lying area has led to predictions that one day this beautiful city will sink beneath the waves.

This aerial photograph shows a section of Venice, highlighting the Grand Canal and the many smaller canals that lead off from it.

Discussing the photograph
▶ Show the children the aerial photograph of Venice and give them time to look carefully. Explain that this is what Venice looks like from an aeroplane. Ask open questions about what they can see on the picture.
▶ Discuss how this perspective is similar to a map and how an aerial picture can help us to find where places are. Point out the route of the main waterway and tell the children that it is called the Grand Canal, or *Canal Grande* in Italian. Explain that in Italian, *Grande* means 'big'.
▶ Let the children look for and point out other smaller canals, bridges and noticeable large buildings.

Activities
▶ Using a digital camera, take oblique or vertical 'aerial' photographs of classroom objects, or small LEGO models of buildings made by the children. This will help to establish

understanding of the 'view from above'. Show the children how to draw round the shapes on the vertical photos to make a plan of the object or model.
▶ Look at and discuss a simple aerial view of a familiar place such as the school or the local area.
▶ Project the aerial view of Venice onto a screen, a large sheet of white paper or the interactive whiteboard and show the children how to draw round the shapes to make a plan of the main canals and features (it will not be an exact map because this is an oblique photograph).

The Grand Canal, Waterbus

These two views of the Grand Canal show how Venice caters to the tourist industry and how people travel around Venice in gondolas and waterbuses. The gondolas are like taxis in most other cities.

Discussing the photographs
▶ Explain that the Grand Canal is like a main road through Venice. Encourage the children to name, locate (using vocabulary such as *left*, *right* and *background*) and describe the features they can see.
▶ Draw attention to the buildings. Why do they have shades on the windows and shop fronts?
▶ Discuss the different types of boats. How many types are there? How do they move? Who is in the boats and what are they doing?
▶ Explain that the small boats are called gondolas. Gondolas take tourists to see the city. The man who rows them is called a gondolier – he is like a taxi driver in our country.
▶ What do the children think the poles in the water are for? Explain that they are used to tie up the boats and to stop the boats knocking against each other. There are hundreds of poles because so many people need to have a boat instead of a car to move around.
▶ Focus in on the waterbus (centre left). It is carrying a lot of passengers. Why does it need to have a roof? Ask the children to find the waterbus stop.
▶ Show the close-up picture of the waterbus reaching the next stop. Help the children to notice that there is no road or even pavement in front of the buildings – if you want to go into them you have to take your boat right up to the arches.

Activities
▶ Give the children pieces of appropriately coloured paper cut into the shape of Venetian buildings. Using the photographs as references, let the children add details to the buildings such as arches, doors, windows and shutters.
▶ Add sloping blinds in bright-coloured card, attached by a folded section at the top to give a 3-D effect.
▶ Help the children to mount the buildings along a canal made from shiny blue or crinkled tissue paper, leaving room for boats to be added later.
▶ Ask the children to write a short description of a journey along the canal by waterbus, water taxi (vaporetto) or gondola. Add these to the display.

Water ambulance

In a city where there are few connections by road everything revolves around water transport. This means that all the services needed by a large city have to be adapted to travel by boat and these boats have to take account of the narrowness of some canals and the height restriction of the hundreds of small pedestrian bridges. Venice has thousands of small working boats on which tradesmen carry their tools and supplies. There are delivery boats and an array of public service boats such as ambulances, police boats and waste disposal boats. Canal cleaning is carried out by boats that filter out rubbish as they travel the canals.

Discussing the photograph
▶ Ask the children to name any special vehicles we have in our towns to do important jobs (such as buses, delivery vans and fire engines). Scribe their ideas in a long list. Explain that in Venice all these vehicles would need to go on water.
▶ Show the children the picture of the water ambulance. Ask them to suggest other jobs that boats will need to do.

Activities
▶ Let the children choose an emergency services vehicle in the UK and think about what it looks like. Ask them to redesign their chosen vehicle as a boat and write a few lines about the work it does. How will it help the people of Venice?
▶ Make a classroom display with the children's boats and writing (or add these to the canal frieze).

Video: A gondola ride

The video sequence shows several gondolas taking tourists along a busy stretch of canal and under a little bridge, also busy with tourists. The dress and work of the gondolier can be observed in detail. You can observe how the gondolier uses a single oar and careful positioning to make the gondola more manoeuvrable – vital in busy, narrow canals.

Discussing the video clip
▶ Ask the children to watch the sequence carefully several times. How do the gondolas move? Who is moving and steering them? What is the gondolier using to manoeuvre the boat? Who is in the boat and why are these people in Venice?
▶ Explain that when the gondolier pushes the oar forward the water is pulled back and the boat moves forward. By changing the position of the oar and the strength of the pull the gondolier can control how the boat moves.
▶ The gondolas are approaching a low and narrow bridge. Where will they need to be to get under the bridge? Do the children notice any patterns in the way the gondolas are manoeuvred?

Activities
▶ Role-play the action seen in the video clip. Choose children to take on the roles of gondoliers, tourists, workmen and pedestrians. Ask the groups to explain where they are going and why, what they can see and hear and what they think and feel about Venice.
▶ Use the word GONDOLA to make a class acrostic poem, describing the things they would see on a trip through Venice.
▶ Let the children, working in small groups with classroom assistants, design posters advertising a gondola trip which tells tourists about the sights of Venice.

Living in Venice, Shopping in Venice

As well as a holiday destination, Venice is also a place where ordinary Italians live and work. These photographs show typical scenes in the small side canals where normal life goes on. Here the homes have boats rather than cars parked outside and market stalls are set up on barges rather than roadside stalls.

Discussing the photographs
▶ Ask the children how these homes differ from their homes and make a list of the differences.
▶ Discuss how the people must travel to and from their homes.
▶ Consider how the people make sure that the area is as safe as possible for children and animals.
▶ Ask the children where they think people go to shop. How do they get there? How might they carry their shopping home?
▶ Draw attention to the reflections. Why do the buildings look wobbly in the water?
▶ Ask the children what they notice about this market stall. What are the similarities and differences with market stalls in this country?

Activities
▶ Ask the children to draw a part of the school's exterior, and then ask them to draw what they think it would look like if it were reflected in water.
▶ Using the other photographs of Venice, compile sentence cards that describe homes in Venice.
▶ Ask the children to list the similarities and differences of living in Venice and their own locality. Where would they prefer to live and why?

- Set up a pasta and pizza restaurant in the role-play area and encourage the children to act out ordering and making some Italian foods.
- Explore some different dried pasta shapes. Make pictures or Venetian masks using pasta shapes to make facial features. Paint and glaze with diluted PVA adhesive.

NOTES ON THE PHOTOCOPIABLE PAGES

Word cards
PAGES 74–75

These cards show key words that children will encounter when working on the unit:
- words relating to the different locations in Europe
- words to develop geographical vocabulary.

Encourage the children to build their own word bank as they work on the resources.

Activities
- Cut out the cards and laminate them. Use the word cards as often as possible when talking about the features in the resources in this gallery.
- Encourage the children to match the word cards to the pictures in the Resource Gallery.
- Use the word cards to match similar features in pictures about different countries. How are places similar to others?

Learning about Europe
PAGE 76

This activity sheet introduces foreign languages and also helps the children to recognise the shapes of countries and their flags.

Activities
- Teach the children to say 'hello' in the five countries we will visit.
- Play the 'welcome game' – when you hold up each flag the children say 'welcome' in the appropriate language.
- Can the children recognise the shapes of the countries, their flags and their language?

A brave little Dutch boy
PAGES 77–78

This traditional story is about Hans Brinker, the fabled Dutch boy who prevented a flood by stemming a leaking dyke with his finger. The moral behind the story is that by acting quickly, we can avert disasters even if we have limited strength. The story also teaches that a small trickle can become a stream that can become a devastating flood.

This story may be told or read. It is likely that Key Stage 1 children will take the story literally and from this they will begin to understand the problems associated with reclaimed land below sea level that requires artificial barriers to keep out the sea. If, however, the children have already studied fables in their literacy work this story offers a cross-cultural dimension to that work.

Discussing the story
- Read the story to the children. Ask them to recall the main events in the story.
- Consider how Hans felt when he saw the water leaking from the dyke. What might have happened if Hans had not seen it?
- How did Hans help his village? How did the people feel about what Hans did?
- Ask the children if they can think of ways to help people where they live. Write a list of their ideas on the whiteboard.
- If appropriate to the children's understanding, tell the children that this story is a fable and explain simply what it means (a story with a moral or message).

Activities
- Make a set of cards retelling the main events of the story and use these with small groups to reconstruct the correct sequence of events (either verbally or in writing).
- Help the children to make an imaginative pictorial map showing Hans' route home to his village and where he stayed to stop the water.

▶ Ask groups of children to think of other contexts in which water can be a danger to humans. For each one, write a good idea to prevent or minimise the danger.

Heidi at home   PAGE 79

The children's classic *Heidi* by Johanna Spyri (Penguin Popular Classics) offers excellent inspiration for discussing the Alpine environment with young children. Heidi's child's eye view will help young children to learn through empathy with Heidi and comparison with their own lifestyles, making historical as well as geographical comparisons.

Discussing the story
▶ Read the extract about Heidi's first day in the chalet. Explain this was more than 100 years ago.
▶ Talk to the children about why there are still small huts on the mountains today.
▶ Ask the children to recall the layout and equipment in Heidi's chalet. Encourage them to contrast this with their own homes.
▶ What jobs do the children think grandfather and Heidi needed to do each day?
▶ Ask the children to close their eyes and imagine the view from Heidi's bedroom window.
▶ Talk about how winter would change the landscape where Heidi lived.

Activities
▶ Together, make a list of the features of the main room in Heidi's chalet. Ask the children to draw a simple, labelled pictorial map of this layout.
▶ Let the children make pastel drawings or paintings of Heidi's chalet in the summer and in the winter. Using light blue sugar-paper as a background will make it easier for them to show snowy mountains against a blue sky.
▶ Let the children experiment with short lengths of art straws or sticks to build a chalet-style building.
▶ Draw up two columns headed 'Grandfather's jobs' and 'Heidi's jobs' and ask for suggestions for the lists. What jobs do the children do at home? Do they think Heidi's life was easier or harder than their own?

Heidi's first day   PAGE 80

Heidi goes to live with her grandfather because there is no one else to look after her. She makes friends with Peter, a goatherd, who lives further down the mountain. He teaches Heidi to love nature and appreciate the beauty of the Swiss landscape.

Discussing the story
▶ Read the extract and ask the children to recall what Heidi could see from the mountainside. How do they think Heidi felt about the view?
▶ Show the children pictures of alpine meadow flowers (from brochures or from the internet). Talk about the colours and shapes of the flowers and tell the children the names of some of the flowers.
▶ Explain that many people go to Switzerland to see the wildflowers and that people take care of them and do not pick them. Discuss why we should all take care of wildflowers. Consider what would happen to the countryside if we picked them.
▶ Ask the children to recall how Heidi learned this lesson.

Activities
▶ Make a class Alpine meadow picture using printing techniques and collage to obtain a 3-D effect. Cut out a sloping hillside in pale green sugar-paper and stick this onto a large sheet of light blue backing paper. Have adult helpers working with groups to print flower and leaf shapes using potato cuts to make the background while others make flowers with art straw stems and coloured and textured paper leaves and petals. Fix the flowers onto the display and add a caption to make a poster urging people to protect wild flowers.
▶ Use small pictures of wildflowers or other features of the Swiss landscape as stimuli for descriptive prose or poetry writing. Use the geography key questions – *What is it? Where is it? What is it like? How do I feel about it?* as a framework for thinking about the content of the writing.

Europe word cards

TRAIN RIDE THROUGH EUROPE

canal	valley
windmill	snow
countryside	steep
mountain	slope
river	grass
waterfall	track

Europe word cards

TRAIN RIDE THROUGH EUROPE

barge	gondolier
bicycle	shade
train	bridge
gondola	water taxi
oar	water bus

Learning about Europe

TRAIN RIDE THROUGH EUROPE

Italy			buongiorno	arrivederci
Germany			guten tag	auf wiedersein
Holland			hallo	vaarwel
France			bonjour	au revoir
UK			hello	goodbye

76

SCHOLASTIC PHOTOCOPIABLE

READY RESOURCES ▶▶ GEOGRAPHY

A brave little Dutch boy (1)

TRAIN RIDE THROUGH EUROPE

Once upon a time on a farm in the flat countryside of Holland, lived an eight-year-old boy called Hans. He lived with his father and mother in a small farmhouse. It had a small pretty garden filled with flowers, set on a flat polder where his father's cows grazed on the grass and where beautiful tulips grew in brightly coloured rows every spring. Their house had its own blue and white windmill with red sails. The windmill pumped water from the land when it was too wet. The village where Hans lived was kept safe from floods from the canal by a high mound of earth called a dyke, which stopped the canal water running onto the fields in wet weather. This dyke had been built by all the people in the village to keep the water away from their farms. They were always afraid that the water would break through the dyke and flood their homes and drown their animals! They did not feel safe without the dyke and were worried in case the 'evil water' came too near their homes.

Hans was a kind boy who loved to help people. One autumn day he set out to take some of his mother's best biscuits to a poor old blind man who lived on the other side of the dyke. On his way he noticed how full the canal was and wondered whether it might overflow, but it was a fine, sunny day so he did not worry.

The old man was very pleased with his biscuits and Hans chatted happily to his old friend until it was almost dark. Then he said goodbye and set off to walk back along the dyke, to his own home where his supper would be ready for him.

Suddenly the sky became dark, the wind blew in his face and heavy rain began to fall. Hans began to run in case it became so dark and rainy that he could not see his way home. Every so often he stopped and looked anxiously across the fields for his own windmill, but the wind and rain were so strong that he could hardly see his way.

Then Hans heard a frightening sound. He stopped and listened carefully. There was no mistaking the noise of water

A brave little Dutch boy (2)

TRAIN RIDE THROUGH EUROPE

dripping and trickling. 'It must be the evil water!' he whispered, although there was not a person nearby, nor even a grazing cow to hear him. Hans could barely see the dyke in the dim light. He followed the sound of the dripping water, searching with his eyes and feeling the dyke until at last he felt the wet trickle. Then, beneath his fingers, he felt a rush of water streaming through a small hole in the dyke.

Hans knew that unless the water stopped a small hole would soon become a big hole and a little trickle of water could become a great flood. This might fill the fields and drown the animals and even reach as far as his village. It could destroy the pretty gardens, the painted houses and even his lovely windmill. At that moment Hans knew exactly what he must do.

He pulled his coat around him and sat down by the dyke in the darkness. He carefully placed his finger into the little hole and stopped the trickling water … and there he sat, hour after hour, through the dark rainy night, very cold, very hungry and very, very scared. He watched and waited, and waited and watched until at last the sky began to lighten and the dim shapes of the houses and windmills could be seen across the flat polder. Brave little Hans was numb with cold, but the homes and families were safe. Soon he was found by a passerby and the men of his village came with their tools to made the dyke strong again.

Hans was a hero and his story has been told for over one hundred and fifty years. It shows just how much bravery and love children can show towards their families, their communities and their country.

Re-written by Liz Lewis from a story by Mary Elizabeth Mapes Dodge in 1865.

Heidi at home

TRAIN RIDE THROUGH EUROPE

Grandfather's home was a good-sized room which covered the whole ground floor of the hut. A table and a chair were the only furniture. In one corner stood her grandfather's bed, in another was the hearth with a large kettle hanging above it and on the farther side was a large door in the wall – this was the cupboard. Her grandfather opened it. Inside were his clothes: some hanging up; others, a couple of shirts and some socks and handkerchiefs, lying on a shelf. On a second shelf were some plates, cups and glasses, and on a higher one still there was a round loaf, smoked meat and cheese. He kept everything needed for his food and clothing in this cupboard. Heidi, as soon as it was opened, thrust in her bundle of clothes.

She then looked carefully around the room. 'Where am I to sleep, Grandfather?'

'Wherever you like,' he answered.

Heidi was delighted and began at once to examine all the nooks and corners to find out where it would be pleasantest to sleep. In a corner near her grandfather's bed she saw a short ladder against the wall. Up she climbed and found herself in the hayloft. There lay a large heap of soft, sweet-smelling hay, while through a round window in the wall she could see right down the valley.

'I shall sleep up here, Grandfather,' she called down to him. 'It's lovely up here. Come up and see how lovely it is!'

After eating a delicious supper of bread, toasted goat's cheese and warm goat's milk, Heidi settled down for the night and slept soundly until dawn. She was wakened by a loud whistle. She climbed down the ladder and ran outside the hut.

Illustration © TDR (Birmingham). Text: edited extract by Liz Lewis from *Heidi* by Johanna Spyri (1880)

Heidi's first day

TRAIN RIDE THROUGH EUROPE

The next day Heidi joined Peter the goatherd to take her grandfather's goats to graze on the mountain...

She started joyfully for the mountain. During the night the wind had blown away all the clouds; the dark blue sky was spreading overhead and in its midst was the bright sun shining down on the green slopes of the mountain, where the flowers opened their little blue and yellow cups. Enchanted with this waving field of brightly coloured flowers, Heidi forgot even Peter and the goats. She began to pluck whole handfuls of flowers and put them into her little apron, for she wanted to take them all home and stick them in the hay so that she might make her bedroom look just like the meadows outside.

'Come along here,' called Peter. 'You are not to fall over the rocks.' On one side of the mountain the rocks were split into clefts and Peter had reason to warn her of danger.

Heidi unfastened her apron, rolling it carefully round the flowers, and sat down and looked about her. The valley lay far below bathed in the morning sun. In front of her, a broad snowfield rose high against the dark blue sky. Heidi sat without moving, her eyes taking in the whole scene and all around was a great stillness, broken only by soft puffs of wind that swayed the light bells of the flowers, and set them nodding merrily on their slender stems. She had never felt so happy in her life before.

In the evening, when Heidi returned to the chalet, she showed her grandfather what she had brought for him. Opening the apron that held her flowers she shook them all out at her grandfather's feet. But the poor flowers, how changed they were! Heidi hardly knew them again. They looked like dried bits of hay, not a single flower cup stood open.

'Oh Grandfather, what is the matter with them?' exclaimed Heidi in shocked surprise. 'They were not like that this morning, why do they look so now?'

'They like to stand out in the sun and not be shut up in an apron,' said her grandfather, wisely.

'Then I will never gather any more,' Heidi sadly replied.

Text: edited extract by Liz Lewis from *Heidi* by Johanna Spyri (1880)